Mom

love you,
Janna + Gary
2014

PREPARE

SPIRITUAL AND FINANCIAL READINESS
FOR THE COMING ECONOMIC STORM

PREPARE

ETHAN POPE

Intersect Press
Dallas, Texas

Learn more at www.PrepPlan.org

PREPARE: Spiritual and Financial Readiness for the Coming Economic Storm

Copyright © 2014 by Ethan Pope

Intersect Press: *Bringing Truth and People Together*
ISBN 978-0-9826470-2-8

PREPARE is a follow-up to *America's Financial Demise: Approaching the Point of No Return*, published in 2010 (based on 2009 data). PREPARE offers a condensed version of economic data and answers the top two questions from readers of *America's Financial Demise*: (1) How do I prepare for the coming economic crisis, and (2) What is the biblical perspective?

Certified Financial Planner Board of Standards Inc. owns the certification mark CERTIFIED FINANCIAL PLANNER ™ , which it awards to individuals who successfully complete the CFP Board's initial and ongoing certification requirements.

Editor: Dave Lindstedt
Editorial consultant: Natalie Orr
Proofreaders: Austin Pope, Paul Allen, Texas Tucker
Cover design: Kirk DouPonce, DogEared Design – www.DogEaredDesign.com
Interior design: Katherine Lloyd – www.TheDESKonline.com

Note: This book is not intended to give specific, legal, tax, economic, or investment counsel. Neither the author nor the publisher can take responsibility for a reader's decisions based on the data or concepts presented in this book. It is the reader's responsibility to consult with a professional advisor before making any decisions. Due to the changing economic environment, we recommend that you seek professional counsel for your individual circumstances.

The version of Proverbs 27:12 used throughout the book is the author's paraphrase.

Printed in the United States of America

The wise see danger ahead and prepare;
a fool ignores the facts and suffers the consequences.

PROVERBS 27:12

PREP Plan

P REPARE SPIRITUALLY

R EALLOCATE RESOURCES

E CONOMIZE LIFESTYLE

P AY OFF DEBT

www.PrepPlan.org

CONTENTS

INTRODUCTION

The mother of all economic storms is headed our way, yet most Americans seem oblivious to the danger. Despite the gathering thunderclouds of annual federal budget deficits and a rapidly escalating national debt, most people are simply ignoring the news and information concerning the coming economic crisis.

There's really nothing complicated about it. You only need one chart to illustrate our nation's unsustainable course.

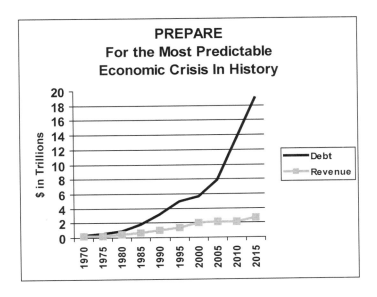

Clearly, we are living on a "debt bubble" that is rapidly expanding. And we know that *all bubbles eventually burst.* There should be no surprise this time.

Unfortunately, this issue has become politicized in our society, and the partisan divide between liberals and conservatives, Democrats and Republicans grows wider every day. But one of my hopes in this book is to remove all the politics and simply look at the economics of the situation.

We are approaching the point of no return when it will become mathematically impossible for our nation to correct the problem—and, quite frankly, all the speeches, sound bites, and political spin-doctoring are not helping matters one bit. Unless we change course *soon*, we will be brought to our knees economically, militarily, socially, and spiritually. A new world order is on the horizon.

Some people believe that our nation is already past the point of no return, and they have decided to spend their time and money helping other people prepare for the approaching upheaval. Others are working diligently on a political solution. And a few are praying for a miracle. I respect and applaud all three objectives. But no matter what your beliefs, your political affiliation, or your strategies, you need to prepare *now* for the consequences ahead.

You must understand that the issues of our national debt and runaway deficits are no longer just about your kids and grandkids. It's now about you and me, as well. It doesn't matter if you are twenty, forty, sixty, or eighty years old. The timeline has shifted and we all need to take action.

History proves that runaway debt undermines the health and strength of a nation. Need an example? Here are two: ancient Rome and modern-day Greece.

What caused the demise of the Roman Empire? Three things:

- poor fiscal policy
- pride
- moral decay

In other words, they *self-destructed*. America appears to be drawing from Rome's playbook. We are on the exact same path.

But we have something the Romans didn't have—almost four hundred years of Christian heritage and faith in a God who is able to redeem and restore even the most hopeless-seeming circumstances. As we'll see, that's not something to be taken for granted.

What about the modern-day crisis in Greece? If you study the data, you will see three primary problems: (1) unrestrained government spending; (2) a growing national debt; (3) a downgraded credit rating, leading to rising interest rates, resulting in an inability to service their debt.

In 2010, when I published *America's Financial Demise*, the feedback I received from readers fell into four categories that have influenced my writing of *PREPARE*:

- Some people said there was too much data; that it was overwhelming and depressing, and that my tone was too harsh.
- Others said I hadn't done enough to develop a biblical perspective on the threats facing our nation. They wanted to know more about how a Christian worldview intersects with the issues of our day.
- Related to that feedback was a desire expressed by some to see more about opportunities for ministry, despite— or perhaps because of—our dire circumstances. They wanted to see more *hope*, as befits a people whose faith is in God.
- And people wanted to know more about how to prepare—how to protect their assets and how to be ready to help others in times of need.

I have done my best to address these concerns in the pages that follow, and I invite you to not only read, but also *apply*, the principles and strategies you'll find in the nineteen chapters of this book.

Before you turn the page and begin chapter 1, I have a few important things I want you to know and understand about this book:

- First of all, it's important to understand that *both* political parties are responsible for decades of fiscal policy decisions that have put our nation on an unsustainable course. You will not get any political spin from me. There's plenty of blame to go around, and we're all in this together.

- That said, we must tone down the rhetoric and eradicate the political bias if we hope to have any chance of solving the problem. Since when did being rude, yelling, and belittling people ever accomplish anything—except to create hard feelings between people? We need to bring civility back into the public square. It's interesting to note that the first word Webster's New World Dictionary uses to define *civility* is "politeness." So, let's work to put the *polite* back into *politics*.

- Our economic problems are symptoms of our spiritual problems as a nation. *PREPARE* is written from a biblical worldview.

- The Bible is our source for how to understand and approach events such as life and death; prosperity and poverty; economic expansion and recession, and even the rise and fall of nations.

- God has not promised perpetual prosperity to any person or nation. This includes the United States of America, contrary to what some people may believe.

- God is powerful enough to change the economic course of our nation if He chooses to answer the prayers of those asking for a miracle.

- We do not know whether God's plan for America includes continued economic prosperity, judgment, or perhaps another spiritual awakening. But I think we're about to find out.

- We need to have a sense of urgency to put our financial house in order (families, businesses, churches, the federal government).

- On the horizon, a global economic storm is gathering that will affect billions of people both spiritually and financially.

- When the economic storm comes ashore, we will have the greatest opportunity for ministry in the history of our nation. *But will we be ready? Will our churches be ready? Will our ministries be ready?*

- When the economic storm comes ashore, I believe we will also have the greatest opportunity for the creation of wealth in the history of our nation.

- We should view any peaceful economic years ahead as a gift of God's mercy, allowing us more time to prepare spiritually and financially. But it would be foolish to assume we still have plenty of time to get ready. We must begin to prepare *now* for the coming crisis.

- We must be like "the sons of Issachar, men who understood the times, with knowledge of what Israel should do" (1 Chronicles 12:32).

- Our first priority is to prepare spiritually.

- Our second priority is to prepare financially.

- *PREPARE* is more about *individual* and *community* preparation than it is about trying to solve all the problems with the federal government, the president, and Congress.

- Once you have put your own house and life in order, you can expand the circle to influence your friends, your city, your state, your nation, and your world. Become a part of the solution and help others prepare.

- "Iron sharpens iron, so one man sharpens another" (Proverbs 27:17). Let the sharpening begin!
- "The wise see danger ahead and prepare; a fool ignores the facts and suffers the consequences" (Proverbs 27:12).

We are facing the most predictable economic crisis in the history of our nation. Why *wouldn't* you prepare?

Prepare now.

PROBLEM

America is on an
unsustainable fiscal course

PREPARE

Chapter 1

PREPARE NOW

We face the most predictable economic crisis in history.
—Erskine Bowles, former chief of staff for President Bill Clinton,
testifying before the Senate Budget Committee, March 8, 2011

pre·pare – *to set in order, to make ready, to equip*
Webster's New World Dictionary

Several years ago, I was on an early morning flight from Chicago to Memphis. The captain came on the intercom and said, "Ladies and gentlemen, we have just lost power in one of our engines. In a few minutes, we will be landing in Evansville, Indiana. Please prepare for landing."

The captain's announcement immediately got everyone's attention, and an eerie silence filled the plane. *Wall Street Journal*s and *USA Today*s were quietly folded and put away, mothers held their babies closer, seat belts were tightened, bags were stored away, and I'm sure everyone had thoughts of loved ones. You could see the concern on the passengers' faces. Everyone understood the urgency of the moment, and everyone was intently listening to the captain's and flight attendants' instructions as we prepared to land.

Well, almost everyone . . .

A few moments after the captain's announcement, I was surprised to hear a passenger laughing. I looked across the aisle and saw a man wearing earphones and watching a movie on his laptop, completely oblivious to the unfolding drama taking place on the plane. Another passenger, seated in the row in front of me, slept through the entire landing and woke up in Evansville thinking he was in Memphis. *Boy, was he shocked!*

Moments after the captain's announcement, one of the flight attendants tapped the movie-watching passenger on the shoulder and informed him of the situation. He quickly removed his earphones, turned off his movie, and prepared for landing. However, the flight attendant let the passenger in front of me continue to sleep.

When I looked out the window as we were landing in Evansville, I noticed that the airport had made preparation for our emergency landing, with ambulances, fire trucks, and other emergency vehicles waiting on the edge of the runway. Thankfully, the plane landed safely, and we avoided disaster. But what might have happened if the pilots had ignored the alarms going off in the cockpit? What if they had seen that the engine had shut down but failed to act on the information immediately?

I've often reflected on my experience during that early morning flight to Memphis; and I have compared the situation—especially the three scenarios that unfolded after the captain's announcement—to the coming global economic crisis.

- Some people are on full alert and have started to prepare for possible emergencies.
- Some people are distracted and disengaged. They're still amusing themselves and are oblivious to the coming dangers. Perhaps a friendly tap on the shoulder will alert them to the need for action.
- Some people are asleep, and quite frankly show no signs of waking up in time.

DISENGAGED, ASLEEP, OR ALERT?

Today, too many Americans can be compared to the man on the plane who was watching the movie—distracted, laughing, and oblivious. *They haven't a clue about the real economic danger we face as a nation.*

Thankfully, someone tapped the man on the shoulder, got his attention, informed him of the captain's announcement, and helped him properly prepare for a potential crisis.

Because I was sitting across the aisle from this man, I heard the entire conversation. I can assure you that he did not ignore or argue with the flight attendant. He immediately forgot about being entertained and became fully engaged in preparing for what lay ahead. *What previously had been important quickly faded away.*

I have often wondered why the flight attendant did not wake up the sleeping passenger to alert him. And I have asked myself many times, "How many people will I be able to tap on the shoulder, get their attention, and help to properly prepare, and how many people will I let continue to sleep? *That's a sobering thought.*

I am deeply burdened that, over the past seven years, as I have been researching and writing, I haven't done more to tap people on the shoulder and urge them to take action.

If you are not already awake and alert, my desire in writing this book is to *tap you on the shoulder* so you will be informed, prepared spiritually and financially for the coming economic crisis, and motivated to begin tapping others on the shoulder, to get their attention and help them prepare.

When the economic storm comes ashore, billions of people around the world will be affected. Why? The economies of most nations are now linked to one other as never before. There has always been a global economy, and the United States has been an important player for the past few centuries. But in recent years, more leverage and speculation has been added to the system, and more categories of risk have been defined. And because much of that leverage, speculation, and risk resides within the American economy, it has created pressure points that have never before existed to this extent. Though other major players—such as China, Japan, and the European Economic Union—have come onstage in recent decades, it's still safe to say that as America goes economically, so goes the world.

At this point in history, America is the first domino, and most powerful domino, in a chain of economic dominos that stretches across the globe. If America falls, every other domino (nation) would be affected in some way. So, this is not just a warning for America, but a global economic warning, for people living in every nation.

Here's what we know and don't know about the coming economic crisis:

- We don't know exactly *how* it is going to happen.
- We don't know exactly *when* it is going to happen.
- But, we do know that it *is* going to happen unless our nation changes course.

It is my hope that, with a genuine sense of urgency, you will grasp this opportunity to prepare spiritually, put your own financial house in order, and help others prepare. Just as the powerful forces of a tsunami travel across the ocean floor and come ashore without warning, the coming economic tsunami will strike suddenly.

I remember more than seven years ago, when I first shared my research, PowerPoint presentation, and concerns about the economy with my wife, daughter, and son, my daughter said, "Dad, why isn't anyone else talking about this?"

Here's how I interpreted her question: "Dad, are you *really* sure about this?"

In the ensuing years, I've asked myself that question *hundreds* of times. "Ethan, are you *really* sure about this? Are we *really* facing

America's financial demise? Even the words sound and look strange, like an oxymoron. *America* and *financial demise* just don't seem to go together.

But we only have to study history to see that other great empires have fallen. And no doubt there was a time when no one could have imagined the demise of, say, the Roman Empire. And yet Rome fell and has never returned to its former glory. And as we've seen, the same three factors that undermined the Roman Empire—poor fiscal policy, pride, and moral decay—are all evident in twenty-first century America. Should we not be concerned that we're on a similar trajectory?

Am I really sure about America's financial demise? The statistical probability is very high, but only God knows what future events will unfold. As deficits continue, as the national debt increases, the answer becomes a more convincing *yes* every year. We are on an unsustainable path.

Still, there's no need to panic, no need to worry, no need to live in fear. We must walk with God every day and trust Him equally in days of economic prosperity and when economic storms come ashore. But we also need to *prepare* for the coming economic crisis. Wise men and women prepare.

In the following chapters, I will make my case that "the *most predictable* economic crisis in history" is on the horizon and heading straight toward you and your family, no matter where you live in the world. An economic storm is in the forecast.

The data I present will be convincing, alarming, and eye-opening. If you are like most Americans, you will have a powerful desire to reject, ignore, or explain away this disturbing new information. I understand. It's called *cognitive dissonance*:

Mental conflict that occurs when beliefs or assumptions are contradicted by new information. . . . When confronted with challenging new information, most people seek to preserve their current understanding of the world by rejecting, explaining away, or avoiding the new information or by convincing themselves that no conflict really exists."[1]

Don't let cognitive dissonance cause you to stop reading and only hear part of the story, or keep watching your movie, or go to sleep.

CHANGE IS ALWAYS DIFFICULT

If you're at all like me, you're probably asking yourself some questions: How can I make this not hurt? How can I avoid dealing with this topic? How can I continue my current lifestyle?

It's naïve to think we can develop a plan that will completely avoid the consequences of our government's mistakes, which have been piling up for decades. When the economic storm arrives, everyone will suffer to some extent. But just because we cannot eliminate suffering in the world does not mean we shouldn't plan to alleviate as much of it as possible. Proverbs 27:12 says, "The wise see danger ahead and prepare; a fool ignores the facts and suffers the consequences."

Here's the good news: Those who plan ahead will be more likely to minimize their suffering and will be better prepared to serve and encourage others.

I believe some people will actually profit financially (increase their wealth) during and after the economic storm. Why? Because they were *wise, understood the times, looked ahead,* and *prepared.* Through careful planning, they will put themselves in a position to profit—even during hard economic times.

You might be surprised to learn that not all families lost wealth during the Great Depression in the 1930s. Some families actually increased their wealth and became millionaires.

Here's something else to keep in mind: By God's sovereign will, you were ordained to live during *this* era of human history (Psalm 139:16). Just like Joseph (Genesis 45:4-8); Nehemiah (Nehemiah

2:17-18); Esther (Esther 4:14); and Jeremiah (Jeremiah 1:5) were given specific assignments in their day, God has specific assignments for you during these times. What an exciting time to be alive!

BE FAITHFUL. WORK HARD. PREPARE.

Put your hope in God and view every day—whether it's a day of prosperity or a day of economic storm—as an opportunity for God to use you for His purposes.

Beginning in chapter 11, we will develop a preparation plan (aptly called the PREP Plan). But before I teach you *how* to prepare, I want you to understand *why* you need to prepare.

In chapters 2–10, my goal is to provide important historical data, realistic projections, and personal commentary that will document the somber economic condition of our nation. You will find enough facts and figures to convince you there is a real problem, but my hope is not to overwhelm you.

Let me wrap up this first chapter with a few quick reminders:

- The onset of the Great Depression in 1929 took us by surprise.
- The Savings and Loan crisis in the 1980s caught everyone unaware.
- The 9/11 terrorist attacks stunned us.
- The Wall Street and housing crisis in 2008 blindsided us.

We've been caught off guard before; but when the approaching economic crisis arrives, *surprise* will not be a word that anyone will use. We've known *for years* that this economic crisis was coming.

There will be *no excuses* this time around—only regrets if you have not prepared.

Prepare now.

Chapter 2

SHOULD WE
BE CONCERNED?

*This is preeminently the time to speak the truth,
the whole truth, frankly and boldly. Nor need we shrink from
honestly facing conditions in our country today.*
—President Franklin D. Roosevelt, first inaugural address,
March 4, 1933

Over the last eight years, I have discovered an inter-esting phenomenon. Most Americans *sense* that something is wrong, yet they don't *believe* the United States of America can actually go bankrupt. They hear sound bites about the growing national debt and uncontrollable government spending, yet they have never taken the time to look at the *evidence* that our course is precarious and unsustainable. As a result, most Americans are not motivated to prepare for the coming economic storm. *Most Americans have not honestly faced the facts and acknowledged the truth about the condition of our nation today*.

Let me put it another way: It appears that most Americans have a sound-bite level of knowledge about the situation, but not a life-altering *understanding*. We only put into practice (take action on) what we know to be true based on factual data. So, if we're not convinced there's a real problem, we won't act.

In the next seven chapters you will find an easy to read and understandable summary of thousands of pages of research (charts, quotes, projections). It is information drawn primarily from the government's own websites, and it clearly documents the *unsustainable* deficits, *unsustainable* growth in the national debt, *unsustainable* expansion of our monetary base (that is, the *unsustainable* printing of additional dollars by the government), and *unsustainable* historically low interest rates.

In a 2008 report to Congress, the Government Accountability Office made the situation quite clear: "By definition, something that is unsustainable will *stop*—the challenge is to take action *before* being forced to do so by some sort of crisis."[2]

So, according to the GAO report, if we don't take the necessary action to head off the inevitable consequences of our current circumstances, at some point in the future the U.S. and global economies will simply stop functioning and shut down. Do you want to learn why this is possible and be able to explain it to your family and friends? *Read on.*

THREE TERMS THAT EVERYONE MUST UNDERSTAND

As we begin to look at the economic data, there are three terms that everyone must understand: *budget surplus*, *budget deficit*, and *national debt*. Each fiscal year, when the accounting books are closed on September 30, the federal government ends the year with either a budget *surplus* or a budget *deficit*:

- A *budget surplus* is when government revenues (that is, taxes paid by you and me) *exceed expenses* for the current year. (That's good!)

- A *budget deficit* is when government expenses (all the money the government spends) *exceed revenues* for the current year. (That's not good!)

- The *national debt* is the total amount our nation owes its creditors (domestic, foreign, and intragovernmental lenders and investors). This figure includes all previous deficits (plus interest owed on all outstanding bonds) minus any payments the federal government has made to pay down the national debt.

All during the year, whenever our nation's expenses exceed income, the government pulls out the national credit card and says, "Charge it." This means we finance our debt by selling government bonds (which are promises by the government to pay at some future time) to domestic and foreign investors (such as bond-market investors and other countries, such as China and Japan.) When we overspend (that is, have a budget deficit) we have to borrow money (by issuing more bonds) and the national debt increases.

U.S. Government, Fiscal Year: *

Revenue:	$2.45 trillion (2012)	$2.77 trillion (2013)
Expenses:	$3.54 trillion (2012)	$3.45 trillion (2013)
Deficit:	$1.09 trillion (2012)	$680 billion (2013)

* U.S. Department of Treasury

Don't let the recent decrease in the annual deficit lead you to believe we are now on the right course. The Congressional Budget Office (CBO) has projected that annual deficits will continue to decrease until 2015 and then begin to increase in 2016 heading back toward trillion dollar deficits by 2023. The current decrease in the deficit will only be short-term.[5]

OUR FORTY-YEAR TRACK RECORD

As you examine the chart below, please note that the *surplus* years are those above the "0" line and the *deficit* years are those below the "0" line.

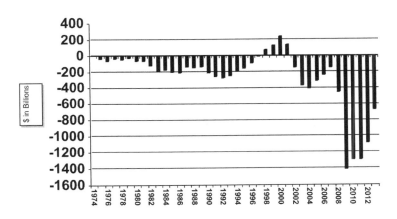

U.S. Federal Budget
40 Year History

Source: Congressional Budget Office (www.cbo.gov) Historical Budget Data

---

FACT: Our nation has had a *budget deficit* in 36 of the last 40 years. That's *90 percent.*

As President Franklin D. Roosevelt said, "Any government, like any family, can for a year spend a little more than it earns. But you and I know that a continuation of that habit means the poorhouse."[6]

FACT: In fiscal year 2012, for every $1 the U.S. Government received in revenue, it spent $1.45.

We often hear Congressional leaders (in both parties) say they are committed to reduce spending, but they haven't yet proved it. Up to this point, it has been all talk with little or no action. Or, as we say in Texas, "All hat and no cattle."

BOTH PARTIES ARE RESPONSIBLE

Despite what you may have heard in the news, there is *no political slant* to the soaring deficit: Since the end of World War II, the budget shortfall has grown under six Republican and six Democratic presidents; it has grown when the Democrats have controlled Congress and when the Republicans have controlled Congress; and even the twelve years of budget surplus (1947–1949, 1951, 1956–1957, 1960, 1969, 1998–2001) are almost equally split between the parties' control of the White House and Congress.[7] Bottom line, there's no point in pointing fingers. We're in this mess together and we need to work together to prepare the coming economic storm.

Our current economic problems are not the result of one piece of legislation, one president, or one session of Congress. Our current economic woes are the cumulative result of a long series of fiscal policy decisions over many, many years. Let's take a brief survey of American history since the Franklin Roosevelt Administration as it relates to fiscal policy:

- **Franklin Roosevelt:** *creation of Social Security and partial removal of U.S. currency from the gold standard.* From the very beginning of Social Security, revenue from payroll taxes has been used to pay benefits to retired people. Excess payroll tax receipts were supposed to be deposited into a Social Security Trust Fund to help pay for future retirement benefits, but as we'll see in chapter 7, the Trust Fund has no money in it. This financial model is unsustainable over the long term.

- **Lyndon Johnson:** *creation of Medicare.* Medicare is a national health care program designed to provide health

30

insurance to Americans over the age of sixty-five. Medicare is headed for bankruptcy.

- **Richard Nixon:** *removed U.S. currency from the gold standard.* The U.S. dollar is now worth less every year in purchasing power and is on course to eventually become worthless.

- **Jimmy Carter:** *economic chaos.* During the Carter Administration, we saw high unemployment (7.8 percent), high inflation (14.8 percent), and high thirty-year mortgage rates (16.32 percent), as well as the energy crisis.

- **Ronald Reagan:** *beginning of unprecedented expansion of budget deficits.*

- **George H. W. Bush:** *continuation of unacceptable deficits.*

- **Bill Clinton:** *expansion of government-backed, subprime mortgages.* The U.S. government is now responsible for approximately $5 trillion in mortgages.

- **George W. Bush:** *expansion of the federal government.* Unprecedented and unacceptable annual deficits exceeding $500 billion for first time. President Bush signed into law an unfunded senior citizen prescription drug plan, stimulus checks, corporate bailouts, and two unfunded wars.

- **Barack Obama:** *trillion dollar deficits.* During the Obama Administration, we've seen corporate bailouts, national health insurance (Obamacare), and unprecedented trillion dollar deficits from 2009–2012. The national debt will more than double during Obama's two terms.

So, you can see that every president over the past eighty-one years has contributed to our current situation. *No president or political party gets an award for fiscal responsibility.*

I firmly believe we should hold our elected leaders accountable for their actions, but the evaluation must begin *first* in my own life. What have I done to escalate the problem or solve the problem? Is my own financial house in order? If my financial house is in order (and it doesn't have to be *perfect*), then I have a responsibility to speak up. But if my financial house is *not* in order, that's where I need to begin. I encourage you to take a look at your own situation and start there.

PREPARE is more about *you and me* than it is about our elected officials. It's more about *individual and community preparation* than it is about trying to solve all the problems with the federal government, the president, and members of Congress.

How do we change our nation? One person, one family, at a time. We begin by taking personal responsibility. Then we seek to enlarge the circle, to inform and influence our neighbors, our cities, our states, and eventually our country and the world. But it all begins with you and me (see Acts 1:8 for a biblical model).

IS OUR PROBLEM *ECONOMIC* OR *SPIRITUAL*?

I believe that what is troubling our nation is not primarily an economic problem. It's a *spiritual* problem. Our economic problems are *symptoms* of our spiritual problem.

When there is moral rot within a nation, its government topples easily. But wise and knowledgeable leaders bring stability.
Proverbs 28:2, NLT

When the godly are in authority, the people rejoice. But when the wicked are in power, they groan.
Proverbs 29:2, NLT

Upright citizens are good for a city and make it prosper, but the talk of the wicked tears it apart.
Proverbs 11:11, NLT

Without wise leadership, a nation falls.
Proverbs 11:14, NLT

"Don't say such things," the people respond. "Don't prophesy like that. Such disasters will never come our way!"
Micah 2:6, NLT

Be honest. When you were reading these verses, *who* were you thinking about? Democrats? Republicans? George W. Bush? Barack Obama? The U.S. Congress?

We should not be too quick to focus on our elected officials and political parties as the source of all our fiscal problems. Jesus says that we first need to evaluate our own lives and take some personal responsibility:

"Why do you look at the speck that is in your brother's eye, but do not notice the log that is in your own eye? Or how can you say to your brother, 'Let me take the speck out of your eye,' and behold, the log is in your own eye? You hypocrite, first take the log out of your own eye, and then you will see clearly to take the speck out of your brother's eye."
Matthew 7:3-5

As we'll see when we get to the chapters on preparation, the process begins with *us*. Only when individuals and communities begin to prepare will the effects be felt at the state and national level. It only takes a few charts and a little common sense to see that we are on an unsustainable course as a nation. But the road back to sanity and fiscal responsibility runs right through our own front doors.

Should we be concerned about the big picture? Yes, we should be *very* concerned. But the place to *act first* is in our own homes, neighborhoods, churches, and towns.

Prepare now.

Chapter 3

DOES THE GROWING NATIONAL DEBT *REALLY MATTER?*

There are two ways to enslave a nation.
One is by the sword. The other is by debt. [8]
—President John Adams (1797–1801)

Have you (or someone you know) ever been so deeply in debt that you don't have enough monthly income to make your monthly payments? Ever feel enslaved or trapped by your finances? It appears this is where our nation is heading.

People go broke.
Companies go broke.
Nations go broke.
Debt brings families to their knees.
Debt brings nations to their knees.

On September 30, 2013, our national debt was $16.73 trillion.[9] Let me spell that out for you: $16,738,183,526,697. By January 1, 2014, it had grown to $17,315,970,784,950, a 3.45 percent increase in only *three months*.

Let me explain why our growing national debt, which currently exceeds $17 *trillion*, really matters.

1. *When you see the term "national debt," it refers to public debt and intragovernmental debt. Our "national debt" is the total amount of money our government owes. The public portion (about $12 trillion) is owed to private investors (U.S. and around the world) and other nations (who have invested in U.S. Treasury bonds). The intra-governmental debt (about $5 trillion) is money owed to U.S. governmental agencies (Social Security Administration; Civil Service Retirement Fund; Military Retirement Fund; Medicare Trust Fund) that have loaned the federal government money.*

   China and Japan are our two largest foreign creditors. As of July 2013, we owe China $1.277 trillion (8 percent of our total debt) and Japan $1.135 trillion (7 percent). There is a common misconception that we owe China practically 100 percent of our debt, but that is not the case.

2. *The national debt is the total of all past federal budget deficits (see chapter 2), plus the compounding interest on the debt, minus any payments made on the debt.*

3. *The U.S. government continually refinances the debt when it comes due, and then borrows more money to pay the interest we owe.*

In the graph below, you can see the actual and projected growth of our national debt. The source of the actual data from 1983–2013 comes from www.treasurydirect.gov. I used the thirty-year historical average debt growth rate of 8.68 percent to project our national debt for the years 2014–2023. I believe this is actually a best-case scenario, because it encompasses years of economic prosperity as well as years of recession. As alarming as it looks, what you see in the chart below is actually a very optimistic projection.

**U.S. National Debt
In Trillions**

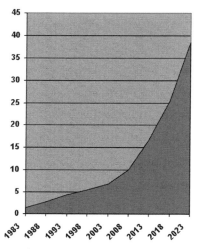

Source 1983–2013: www.treasurydirect.gov
2014–2023: projection based on thirty-year historical average

FACT: The national debt
has not decreased in 56 years.

If you look at the total debt due at the end of each fiscal year (September 30), the amount has not decreased in the past fifty-six years. The last time our debt was lower than the year before was in 1957. Year after year after year, our debt continues to increase. *That's unsustainable.*

Even during the budget surplus years (1998–2001), when Bill Clinton was president and we had a Republican-controlled Congress, we owed more at the end of each year. Yes, we had four budget surplus years (see chart in chapter 2), but those additional funds were not used to pay down the national debt. (You can verify this for yourself at www.treasurydirect.gov, which is a U.S. government website.)[10]

Occasionally, our national debt might decrease during a given year, but it has been more than fifty-six years since the debt was lower at the end of a fiscal year (September 30) than it was at the beginning (October 1 of the previous year).

The March 2009 Government Accountability Office (GAO) *Long-Term Fiscal Outlook* could not be clearer: "The federal government faces *unsustainable growth in debt*."[11] If we do not take action, the report goes on to say, "Eventual changes will be *disruptive* and *destabilizing*."[12]

PROJECTION: The national debt will
more than double in eight short years—
from $10 trillion in 2009 to $20 trillion+ in 2017.

It took our nation *more than 233 years* (1776–2009) to reach $10 trillion in national debt. On January 20, 2009 our national debt was $10.6 trillion. On January 20, 2017 it is projected that our national debt will be over $20 trillion (an increase of more than 100 percent since 2009).

233 years	$10,000,000,000,000 in total debt
8 years	$10,000,000,000,000 in additional debt
	$20,000,000,000,000 or more

What we have is a growing debt tsunami that will one day come ashore.

Alarming.

Unsustainable.

"Why are we experiencing exponential growth in the debt?" The reason is simple—a combination of decades of deficit spending and the negative power of compounding interest.

Prepare now.

Chapter 4

THE NEGATIVE POWER OF COMPOUNDING INTEREST

Albert Einstein said the most powerful force in the universe is compound interest, and today the miracle of compounding interest is working against the federal government.[13]

— Government Accountability Office,
Long-Term Fiscal Outlook, June 17, 2008

Compounding is a powerfully advantageous concept when we are *earning* interest. Examine the following chart, which illustrates how your money will grow and compound if you invest $2,000 at the beginning of each year for forty-five years and earn 10 percent interest per year.*

In the illustration, our total investment is $90,000 ($2,000 x 45 years), but after forty-five years of compounding interest, our investment will be worth more than $1,580,000.

Here's a simple way to understand compounding interest: You are earning interest on your principal *and* earning interest on your interest. For example, during the first year, you earn $200 interest

---

* I am using a 10 percent interest rate for two reasons: (1) It makes it simpler to explain compounding interest; (2) Over the years, it has not been uncommon for the stock market and mutual funds to earn more than 10 percent some years and less than 10 percent in others. In 2013, most stock-based mutual funds returned more than 10 percent. However, we all know that past performance does not guarantee future results.

on your initial investment of $2,000 ($2,000 x 10 percent = $200). During the second year, you earn interest not only on your second-year investment of $2,000, but also on your initial investment of $2,000 *plus* interest on the first year's $200 interest. So in the second year, you will earn $420 interest ($4,200 x 10 percent = $420). As time passes, the amount of accrued "interest on your interest" becomes astronomical.

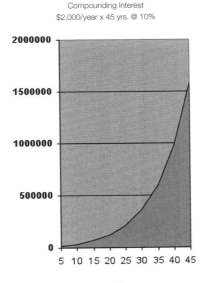

Compounding Interest
$2,000/year x 45 yrs. @ 10%

With compounding interest, there comes a point when the growth curve for your investment begins a rapid ascent. This is the moment you've been waiting for! This is when you can pump your fist and say, "Yes!" because the return on your investment is now compounding at an exponential growth rate. The interest you earn each year now far exceeds the amount of your annual investment. So, in year forty-five of our example, you would invest $2,000 of new money, but your investment account would earn $143,580 in interest!

Stop and think about that: In year forty-five, your investment account would earn $143,580 in interest alone. Why? Because of the cumulative (snowballing) effect of compounding interest.

Here's the alarming news, as it pertains to our national debt: *The same principle of compounding interest works in reverse if you are borrowing money.* If you are a borrower, like the United States, that same power of compounding interest is working *against* you. If you never pay down the principal, and if you borrow money to pay the interest (which is what our nation does every year), eventually it becomes *mathematically impossible* to pay off the escalating debt.

Take a minute to compare the growth curve for the national debt (see the chart on page 36) with the growth curve on the compounding interest chart above. Amazingly similar, right? Both charts take a dramatic upward turn around the 20- to 25-year mark. That's *great* news for an investor and *terrible* news for a borrower.

Compounding interest can lead to financial ruin if you are the borrower. Compounding interest is like a tsunami. The tidal wave of debt begins to swell beneath the surface and one day comes crashing ashore.

One reason why millions of Americans file for bankruptcy each year is because they've made minimum payments on their debts, month after month and year after year, until the compounding interest reached the point of no return and they could no longer service the required debt payment each month. In other words, it became mathematically impossible for them to repay the debt. The same is true for nations. Just look at Greece.

Our nation is on an unsustainable course because of deficit spending and the power of compounding interest working *against* us.

Theoretically, there will come a time when our annual interest payments exceed our total tax revenues. *Practically speaking*, this will never happen, but only because the system will crash long before we ever reach the point where interest expense equals or exceeds one hundred percent of revenues.

On September 30, 2013, the average interest rate on our national debt was 2.43 percent, and we paid $416 billion in interest in fiscal year 2013.[14]

What would happen if our average annual interest rate returned to the long-term historical average rate of about 6 percent?[15] The annual interest due on a debt of $17 trillion would be $1.02 trillion ($17 trillion X 6.00 percent = $1.02 trillion). And remember, in FY2013, total revenues were only $2.4 trillion.

Now, what if the average interest rate shot up to 11.54 percent? Annual interest payments on $17 trillion at 11.54 percent would equal $1.96 trillion. ($17 trillion X 11.54 percent = $1.96 trillion) Compare *that* to total revenues of $2.4 trillion. Alarming, isn't it? If that were to happen, I think we would all agree that a global economic meltdown would soon follow.

You might be thinking, *Hey, Ethan, you can pull whatever numbers you want out of the air and apply them to your equation, but what are the chances of interest rates spiking to 11.54 percent? Haven't they been at historic lows for the past several years?*

Yes, the Federal Reserve has kept interest rates artificially low for the past several years, but there is no guarantee that rates will remain low in years to come. As recently as October 1981, the average interest rate on our national debt was 11.54 percent.[16]

Here's what I want you to understand: **Our nation is sitting on top of an interest-rate time bomb.** Returning to historical average interest rates of only 6 percent would create a global economic crisis. I don't believe there's any question that rates will eventually return to 6 percent or higher; the only question is *when*?

WHY ARE INTEREST RATES SO LOW?

Earlier, I mentioned a common misconception that China holds most of our debt. The truth is that the Chinese hold about 8 percent of our total debt. So, if China isn't buying most of our debt, and Japan (7 percent) isn't buying most of our debt, and domestic private (31 percent) investors aren't buying most of our debt, *who is*?

The U.S. Federal Reserve. It is estimated that the Federal Reserve is now purchasing 60 to 80 percent of the new debt incurred by the federal government each year.[17] This means that the Federal Reserve is creating money out of nowhere and buying our own debt in order to keep interest rates at historic lows. The Fed is doing this for two reasons: (1) to keep the federal government annual interest rate payments low and decrease the annual deficits; and (2) to stimulate a flat economy. (Low mortgage rates help to stimulate the housing market, low car loan rates stimulate the auto industry, and low interest rates for businesses help to stimulate the economy.)

But here's the problem: *It's an illusion. It's a bubble.* The economy is not self-sustaining; it has become dependent on continual stimulus packages from the federal government: the $168 billion stimulus; the $85 billion AIG bailout; the $700 billion TARP bailout; the $787 billion American Recovery and Reinvestment Act; auto industry (GM and Chrysler) bailout; the Cash for Clunkers program; housing market first-time buyer incentives; and the Fannie Mae and Freddie Mac bailouts; and the list goes on and on and on. The design of our free-market system allows businesses to take calculated risks and either be rewarded with increased wealth or potentially lose everything invested. Contrary to what some people believe, it is not the role of the federal government to provide economic stimulus or to cover every bet at the table.

Like a massive hurricane gathering strength offshore, there is an economic storm hovering and building strength with every passing month and year. We would be better off (in the long run) if we allowed the storm to come ashore now, rather than waiting for it to come in on its own in another five, ten, or fifteen years. Yes, times would be hard, we all would experience pain, but we would be more likely to survive.

If the storm comes ashore five, ten, or fifteen years from now, the likelihood of a strong economic recovery (back to normal) will be diminished.

The federal government is not eliminating the threat of an

economic storm by their actions; they're only *delaying* the arrival of the economic storm while the storm continues to gather strength. In recent years, we've had occasional, and in some cases, persistent, downturns (for example, the recession that took hold in 2008—2009), but the main body of the storm has yet to make landfall.

I believe we should view the next few years as a gift and an opportunity to put our financial house in order before the big storm arrives.

> The single biggest threat to national security
> is the national debt.[18] *
>
> —*Navy Admiral Mike Mullen, chairman of the Joint Chiefs of Staff, August 26, 2012*

The first time I read this quote from Admiral Mullen, I thought, Whoa! Run that by me again? Here we have the chairman of the Joint Chiefs of Staff, the chief military advisor to the president, suggesting that the national debt is a greater threat to national security than Al-Qaeda, Iran, North Korea, China or any other army or terrorist group in the world.

Take a minute and think about that one. We are destroying ourselves from within. We are our own worst enemy because we have put ourselves on the road to economic collapse. We have built our nation's economic structure, funded our military, fought overseas wars, and attempted to stimulate and grow our economy by going into debt, using borrowed money. It reminds me of Proverbs 13:7: "There is one who pretends to be rich, but has nothing."

Let me say it a different way: Whatever strength our nation and our economy seem to have—*it's an illusion.* The "recovery" is a *bubble.* The economy is not self-sustaining; it has become dependent on continual stimulus from the federal government.

To paint the picture in terms of another biblical example, we

---

* Admiral Mullen is not an economist, but as a member of the Joint Chiefs of Staff, he is briefed by experts on economic topics and world events.

have built our nation's economy on shifting sands, not on solid rock (Matthew 7:24-28). It is time to abandon the shifting sands and the unbiblical philosophies of the world and to rebuild our nation's economy on the rock of biblical principles.

Admiral Mullen's statement sums up my argument about the national debt. As it continues to grow at an exponential rate, interest payments will consume more and more of our annual tax revenues, which means we'll have less and less to spend in every department of the federal government, including national security (Department of Defense, Homeland Security, the Secret Service, CIA, FBI).

Prepare now.

Chapter 5

PRIMED
FOR INFLATION

*I*nflation is when the cost of goods and services rises. Or you could say that a dollar buys less than it used to. When I was young, a loaf of bread cost thirty cents, and I could buy a soft drink for a dime. Now a loaf of bread might cost $3 and a soft drink in a vending machine costs a buck. That's inflation. Years ago, I considered purchasing a rental property that was selling for $25,000. Today, that same house would sell for more than $100,000. Why the increase? The value (purchasing power) of a dollar today is less than it was years ago. That's inflation. As we prepare financially for the coming economic storm, we must factor in the effects of inflation.

Before we look at what causes inflation, we need to define three important terms: *monetary base*, *"printing" money*, and *economic growth*.

1. *Adjusted Monetary Base:* "The sum of currency in circulation outside Federal Reserve Banks and the U.S. Treasury, deposits of depository financial institutions at Federal Reserve Banks, and an adjustment for the effects of changes in statutory reserve requirements on the quantity of base money held by depositories."[19]

2. *"Printing" Money:* Money is created in two ways: on a printing press or digitally. When the Federal Reserve buys U.S. Government bonds, they create the needed funds digitally. In other words, to buy $80 billion in bonds, they in effect type "$80 billion" into the computer, hit Enter, and *boom* $80 billion is digitally created. (No, you cannot do this on your home computer.)

3. *Economic Growth:* Economic growth is measured in terms of gross domestic product (GDP). GDP is the total value of all goods and services produced in a nation annually. So, if in a period of one year, a nation's GDP increased from $15 trillion to $15.45 trillion, its rate of economic growth would be 3.0 percent.

WHAT CAUSES INFLATION?

Nations that print money (either digitally or by printing paper currency) without restraint in order to pay debtors or expenses or to purchase their own debt are prone to create inflation or hyperinflation.[20] Too much money flooding into the monetary system (see chart below) without sufficient economic growth (GDP) leads to inflation. Let me explain.

As a general rule, the monetary base should expand only as much as the overall economy expands (GDP). As the theory goes, if the economy (GDP) expands at a growth rate of 3 percent, the monetary base can expand at the same rate (3 percent). If the monetary base expands at a rate greater than the economy is expanding, we can expect the difference between the two growth rates to become the rate of inflation. *In theory*, if the monetary base expands by 5 percent and GDP expands by 3 percent in a period of twelve months, we would eventually expect to see an inflation rate of 2 percent (5 percent – 3 percent = 2 percent).

According to the Federal Reserve's own website, our government has been enlarging the adjusted monetary base at an alarming rate since 2008. Note the normal and acceptable gradual increase between 1990 and 2007 and the unacceptable exponential increase of our monetary base beginning in 2008.

U.S. Adjusted Monetary Base

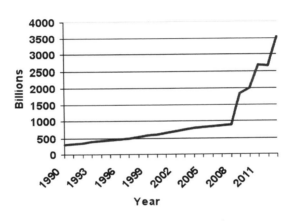

Source: Federal Reserve Bank of St. Louis *

According to the Federal Reserve Bank of St. Louis, our adjusted monetary base, which was $875 billion on September 10, 2008, had expanded to $3.546 trillion by September 18, 2013.[21] This represents an increase of 305 percent in sixty months, or an average annual increase of 61 percent!

To put this enormous expansion of the monetary base in perspective, consider that the increase in the adjusted monetary base during the *previous* sixty months (September 3, 2003– September 10, 2008) was only 16.19 percent.[22] This represents an average annual increase of 3.24 percent—and, I might add, is in line with the annual growth of GDP.

---

* www.research.stlouisfed.org/fred2/series/BASE

During the same five-year period in which the monetary base expanded 305 percent, the economy (GDP) grew by just over 17 percent.[23] If the monetary base does not decline, it would be logical to conclude that we are in store for inflation in excess of 288 percent (305 percent – 17 percent = 288 percent). How does the Fed reduce the monetary base? One option is to sell some of the Treasury Bills they have purchased and then "remove" the digital money from the system.

On May 28, 2008 (which was *before* the massive expansion of the monetary base), Richard Fisher, president of the Federal Reserve Bank of Dallas, offered a warning about the consequences of over-expanding the monetary base:

> We know from centuries of evidence in countless economies, from ancient Rome to today's Zimbabwe, that running the printing press to pay off today's bills leads to much worse problems later on. The inflation that results from the flood of money into the economy turns out to be far worse than the fiscal pain those countries hoped to avoid. . . . Failing to face up to our responsibility will produce the mother of all financial storms. The warning signs have been flashing for years, but we find it easier to ignore them than to take action. Will we take the painful fiscal steps necessary to prevent the storm by reducing and eventually eliminating our fiscal imbalances? That depends on you."[24]

You might be wondering, *How can the Treasury create money out of nothing?*

One reason: Because the U.S. dollar is no longer tied to the gold standard.

First, it is important to understand how the gold standard works.[25] When a nation is on the gold standard, the amount of currency that can be put into circulation is directly linked to the amount of gold held in reserve. (Fort Knox, Kentucky, is home to the

United States Bullion Depository, where much of our nation's gold reserves are stored.) Thus, at any time, the currency in circulation could be converted to physical gold, and the gold backing the currency validates or supports the *value* of the currency.[26]

On April 5, 1933, President Franklin Roosevelt signed Executive Order 6102, which partially removed the U.S. dollar from the gold standard.[27] All American citizens were required to turn in their gold to the United States Treasury. Roosevelt knew that he could not accomplish all the government programs and spending of his New Deal agenda unless he could print more money to pay for everything. He believed it was the role of the federal government to "stimulate" the economy during the Great Depression by spending money on government programs.

This one decision opened the door to excessive government spending and the uncontrolled printing of money. Big government spending programs usually require the ability to freely print more money.

In 1944, most industrialized nations adopted what is known as the Bretton Woods Agreement, which established new rules for international monetary exchange. Many countries fixed their exchange rates to the U.S. dollar because the United States agreed to fix the price of gold at thirty-five dollars per ounce and agreed to exchange U.S. dollars for gold with foreign nations. By the early 1970s, faith in the U.S. dollar had diminished and nations *literally* began shipping dollars to the U.S. and requesting gold in return.

Because the U.S. did not have enough gold to back the U.S. dollars in circulation, President Richard Nixon announced, on August 15, 1971, that the United States would no longer exchange gold for U.S. dollars from other nations or central banks. This event is known as the "Nixon Shock." This unilateral decision by the Nixon Administration spelled the end of any form of gold standard in the world.[*]

---

[*] For more information about the gold standard, you can watch some fascinating video footage of Presidents Roosevelt and Nixon on YouTube. Search for "FDR ends gold standard" and "Nixon ends gold standard" at www.youtube.com.

When a nation's currency is not linked to the gold standard, they have what is called a *fiat currency*. Every nation in the world now operates on fiat currency, which is based on nothing more than the "good faith and credit" of the government issuing the currency.

Fiat currency has value only as long as holders of the currency have faith in the government that issued the money. If that faith diminishes, the currency becomes worthless—possibly overnight.

FIAT CURRENCY

Fiat is a Latin term meaning "let it be done." A fiat currency is declared to be legal tender by the issuing government. Fiat currency is not backed by gold or silver or any other tangible asset.

Hypothetically, what do you think would happen to the purchasing power of the U.S. dollar if the world learned that the United States had increased the money supply not by 300 percent but by 3,000 percent? How much would a single dollar be worth on the world exchange? It would become basically worthless. Such an increase in the money supply without equivalent growth in GDP results in what is called hyperinflation.

In my wallet, I carry around a Zimbabwe 50,000,000,000,000 dollar bill. (That's Z$50 trillion.) It's worthless.

A fiat currency is a crisis waiting to happen, *unless* those who control the printing presses exercise self-control and operate on sound economic principles. (See Richard Fisher's quote.)

Because we are no longer on the gold standard, the Federal Reserve has the ability to create money at will (and *is*).

Unless we begin to chart a new course, it appears that inflation and the demise of the U.S. dollar is just off the coast waiting to come ashore.

Prepare now.

Biblically based, culturally relevant, kindness in speech

The sons of Issachar were men "who understood the times, with knowledge of what Israel should do" (1 Chronicles 12:32).

We need to become like the sons of Issachar. We need to understand the importance and meaning of key terms such as *surplus, deficit, national debt, negative compounding interest, inflation, hyperinflation, monetary base, gold standard* and *fiat currency*.

It is equally important that we understand what the United States should do: We must acknowledge that this is a spiritual problem; return to God; cut spending; eliminate deficits; begin to pay down the national debt; decrease our monetary base; and return to the gold standard (or something similar).

In order to join the debate, we must be (a) biblically based; (b) culturally relevant; and (c) able to clearly articulate the problem, the plan, and what we should do.

When we face opposition, we are never to speak with harsh or mean words, but with grace and kindness. We are to demonstrate love. Know your facts, know your opponent's points and directly address each one, and win him or her over by clearly articulating your position. Your goal is to make any opponent (and those listening to the conversation) thirsty and eager to learn more about God, and your beliefs, by how you live, speak, and treat others.

Do you want a model of how this might look? Read, meditate on, and memorize 1 Corinthians 13:4-8:

> Love is patient, love is kind and is not jealous; love does not brag and is not arrogant, does not act unbecomingly; it does not seek its own, is not provoked, does not take into account a wrong suffered, does not rejoice in unrighteousness, but rejoices with the truth; bears all things, believes all things, hopes all things, endures all things. Love never fails.

Chapter 6

IS SPENDING MORE MONEY *REALLY* THE SOLUTION?

We've gotta go spend money to keep from going bankrupt? . . .
Yes, that's what I'm telling you.
— Vice President Joe Biden, July 16, 2009

On July 16, 2009, Vice President Joe Biden, speaking at a town hall meeting sponsored by AARP, said, "Now, folks, look. AARP knows, and the people with me here today know, the president know[s], and *I* know, that the status quo is simply not acceptable. It's totally unacceptable. And it's completely unsustainable. Even if we *wanted* to keep it the way we have it now, we can't do it financially. We're gonna go *bankrupt* as a nation. Now, people—so, when I say that, people look at me and say, 'What are you talking about, Joe? You're telling me we've gotta go *spend* money to keep from going bankrupt?' The answer is, yes, that's what I'm telling you."[28]

The vice president took some flak for his remarks, but it's important to know there's a name for this kind of thinking. It's called *Keynesian economics.* Keynesian economic theory calls for the government to spend money (it does not have) in order to stimulate growth in the economy. (Check it out on the web by searching "Keynesian economic theory.")

Many people credit Keynesian economics for helping America pull out of the Great Depression. But when you study the data, it becomes obvious that it was WWII that actually caused the economic engine to fire up. Do you want a modern example of how Keynesian economics works? Look no further than the current situation in Greece to find your answer. Bankrupt.

Sometimes, when we start talking about billions and trillions of dollars in the national budget and economy, it's easy to lose track of all the zeros and not fully understand how out of whack everything is at the national level. So, for simplicity's sake, let's break down the numbers from the federal government's fiscal 2012 budget to a level we can all understand: a family budget.

Let's say a friend comes to you for advice on his family's financial situation. Here are the numbers (along with their corollary in the federal budget):

- Total income: $24,000 (government revenues: $2.4 trillion)
- Expenses for mortgage, food, transportation, etc.: $35,000 (government expenditures: $3.5 trillion)
- Amount on credit cards at beginning of year: $148,000 (government debt: $14.8 trillion at beginning of year)
- Amount on credit cards at end of year: $161,000 (government debt: $16.1 trillion at end of year)

Your friend explains that the $13,000 credit card balance increase ($1.3 trillion for government) was due to the family's overspending of $11,000 (government: $1.1 trillion) for expenses. The additional $2,000 (government: $200 billion) was due to *interest on their existing debt.*

What would you think?

You would probably be shocked and alarmed, and you would be thinking, *How can they ever get out of their financial crisis?*

What would you tell your friend to do?

If you are truly a friend, you would tell him to start by doing three things:

- Cut spending—stop buying things they cannot afford
- Live on a balanced budget
- Start paying down their debt.

Common sense tells you that the best plan is to cut spending, balance the budget, and start paying down the debt. But we hear just the opposite from our government.

Should a family facing bankruptcy go on a spending and borrowing spree in order to *save* their family finances? *No, that would be absurd.* But that is exactly what our nation is doing to supposedly solve our nation's fiscal problem.

The laws of economics work the same for any government and family. Overspending, growing debt, and interest payments have already destroyed many families and nations. Just look at ancient Rome, or Greece and Zimbabwe in recent years, if you want some examples.

It's simple mathematics.

There's nothing complicated about it. The numbers just don't add up. Deficit spending and a growing debt bankrupt individuals and nations.

The house of cards cannot remain standing forever. Smoke and mirrors can only hide the truth for so long. An inflated economic bubble will one day burst—and burst suddenly.

Prepare now.

Chapter 7

IS THERE *REALLY* MONEY IN THE SOCIAL SECURITY TRUST FUND?

The federal government will tell you that the Social Security Administration saves surplus payroll tax income every year in order to have sufficient funds to meet the demand for benefits—which has begun to accelerate now that the baby boomers are becoming eligible for retirement benefits (beginning in 2008).

Every year from 1982 to 2009, the amount collected in payroll taxes exceeded the amount paid in benefits. Each year, the surplus went into the Social Security Trust Fund to be used in the future when needed. This is why the Social Security Trust Fund lists assets of $2.6 trillion.

**Social Security Trust Fund
Assets in Trillions of Dollars**

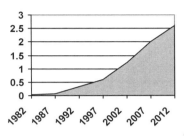

Source: 2013 Annual Report of the Board of Trustees[*]

Unfortunately, those "assets" are not *cash*.

If there's no cash in the bank, where is all the Trust Fund's money? That's a good question! Let's take a look at what has happened to all the payroll tax dollars you and I and everyone else paid into the Social Security system.

Every year in which Social Security had a surplus (payroll tax revenues exceeded benefits paid), here's what happened:

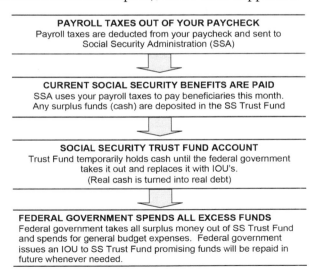

PAYROLL TAXES OUT OF YOUR PAYCHECK
Payroll taxes are deducted from your paycheck and sent to
Social Security Administration (SSA)

CURRENT SOCIAL SECURITY BENEFITS ARE PAID
SSA uses your payroll taxes to pay beneficiaries this month.
Any surplus funds (cash) are deposited in the SS Trust Fund

SOCIAL SECURITY TRUST FUND ACCOUNT
Trust Fund temporarily holds cash until the federal government
takes it out and replaces it with IOU's.
(Real cash is turned into real debt)

FEDERAL GOVERNMENT SPENDS ALL EXCESS FUNDS
Federal government takes all surplus money out of SS Trust Fund
and spends for general budget expenses. Federal government
issues an IOU to SS Trust Fund promising funds will be repaid in
future whenever needed.

---

[*] 2013 Annual Report of the Board of Trustees of the Federal Old-age and Survivors Insurance and Federal Disability Insurance Trust Funds; p.155-156; www.ssa.gov/oact/tr/2013/tr2013.pdf.

So where is the Trust Fund's money? The federal government has spent it *one hundred percent*. There is no cash in the Trust Fund—its only assets are paper (or digital) IOUs from the federal government.

Because Congress has *already spent* every surplus dollar from the Social Security Trust Fund, the United States now must borrow money *every year* in order to repay the IOUs—that is, in order to pay current benefits. Why? It's partly because less revenue is coming in from payroll taxes than is being paid out in benefits. But it's also because there is no cash in the system to draw upon. Instead, the obligation to pay Social Security Trust Fund IOUs must be met from the general budget.

With all its regulatory fervor, the federal government would never allow any private pension fund to hold 100 percent of its assets in debt instruments (IOUs), so why is it acceptable for the Social Security Trust fund to do so?

HERE'S THE PROOF

Remember the debt ceiling debate that Congress had in the summer of 2011? What did they say? Social Security payments could not be mailed unless Congress agreed to raise the debt ceiling. This proves my point that there is no real money in the Social Security Trust Fund.

If there were actual money in the Trust Fund, Social Security checks could be mailed, no problem. In 2011, Social Security benefit payments totaled about $50 billion per month. If there were truly $2.6 trillion in the fund, they could have drawn on that balance to pay the monthly benefits, right? But, there's no money in the Trust Fund, so they have to rely on current borrowing—hence, the pressure on the debt ceiling.

In the summer of 2011, the government had run out of money and could not borrow more to run the government because of the debt ceiling. All the Social Security Trust Fund had was trillions of dollars in IOUs from the government.

Here's the bottom line: Whatever you hear about the sustainability of the Social Security program, if it's based on the size of the so-called Trust Fund, it's a shell game without a pea.

There is no money in the Social Security Trust Fund.

Prepare now.

Chapter 8

THE SHRINKING
WINDOW OF OPPORTUNITY

The federal government faces increasing pressures
yet a shrinking window of opportunity
for phasing in adjustments.[29]
— Government Accountability Office,
Long-Term Fiscal Outlook, June 17, 2008

We are approaching a *critical moment* when we must either begin paying down our national debt or start seeing exponential debt growth, which will lead to bankruptcy.

Here's what the Government Accountability Office (GAO), an independent, nonpartisan agency whose mission is to "support the Congress in meeting its constitutional responsibilities and to help improve the performance and ensure the accountability of the federal government for the benefit of the American people,"[30] says about our current situation:

The passage of time has only worsened the situation: The size of the challenge has grown and the time to address it has shrunk. The longer we wait, the more painful and

difficult the choices will become, and the greater the risk of a very serious economic disruption.[31]
— Government Accountability Office, *Long-Term Fiscal Outlook,*
January 29, 2008

These dates call attention to the narrowing window. . . . Absent action, debt held by the public will grow to unsustainable levels.[32]
— Government Accountability Office, *Long-Term Fiscal Outlook,*
June 17, 2008

The longer action to deal with the nation's long-term fiscal outlook is delayed, the larger the changes will need to be, increasing the likelihood that they will be *disruptive and destabilizing.*[33]
— Government Accountability Office, *Long-Term Fiscal Outlook:*
Fall 2009 Update

With the passage of time the window to address the long-term challenge *narrows* and the magnitude of the required changes grows.[34]
— Government Accountability Office, *Long-Term Fiscal Outlook:*
Fall 2010 Update

If you notice the progression of dates on these quotes, from January 2008 to Fall 2010, it's clear the GAO has been sounding the alarm for some time, and yet Congress has not adequately responded. Let me explain more about this "shrinking window of opportunity."

The following chart documents our national debt since 1983. The projections to 2028 are based on the historical thirty-year (1983–2013) national debt growth rate of 8.68 percent. Using our nation's thirty-year historical debt growth rate is a very reasonable approach to projecting the growth of our national debt. It represents years of great economic growth and also years of economic recession.

As you can see, we are at that "critical moment" (represented by the black circle). The trajectory of the debt is beginning to take off, and it will soon become impossible for our nation to ever pay down or pay off the debt. It is simple arithmetic.

U.S. National Debt
Actual and Projections
In Trillions

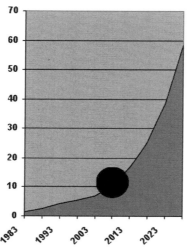

Projected Growth (2014–2028) at 8.68 percent
(Thirty-year historical average)

Don't focus on the exact placement or size of the dot, but on the fact that it represents a small period of time before the debt begins to grow at an exponential rate.

If you think in terms of the height and power of the debt tsunami wave, it's still relatively small in 2014. However, with each passing year of exponential growth in our debt, the potential devastation of the wave increases exponentially.

Here's what Thomas Jefferson, our third president, said about public debt:

> I place economy among the first and most important virtues, and public debt as the greatest of dangers to be feared. . . .

To preserve our independence, we must not let our rulers load us with perpetual debt . . . We must make our choice between economy and liberty or profusion and servitude.[35]

And Erskine Bowles, former chief of staff for President Clinton:

This debt and these deficits that we are incurring on an annual basis are like a cancer. And they are truly going to destroy the country from within.[36]

If we do nothing, by the year 2020, we'll be spending over a trillion dollars a year on interest cost alone.[37]

Here is what concerns me the most about our shrinking window of opportunity: *Even a balanced budget is not enough to solve the problem.*

How many times over the years have you heard a politician say, "*We need a balanced budget amendment*"? In other words, they're saying we need a constitutional amendment voted on by Congress and ratified by two-thirds of the states to *force* Congress to live within their means.

It sounds reasonable and makes for a great sound bite to motivate the political base, but what most people don't realize is that, at this point, even a balanced budget is not enough to solve our fiscal problem.

FACT: Not only do we need to balance the budget, but we need to create a budget surplus in order to have the funds to begin paying down the national debt; or the debt will continue to increase exponentially due to the negative power of compounding interest. The only way to change the trajectory of the debt growth curve is to begin to pay down the principal, which means we must first have a surplus in the budget and stop borrowing money each year to pay the interest.

It's simple arithmetic: One day, the numbers will simply not add up.

It's Economics 101: supply and demand.

It's Budgeting 101: expenses cannot exceed revenues.

It's common sense: The debt will continue to grow, due to compounding interest, until we begin to pay down the principal.

It's understanding how compounding interest works against you when you're a borrower: If you never pay down your debt, you will eventually go broke.

Recently, Congress (Republicans and Democrats) could not even agree on cutting $85 billion out of a $3.5 *trillion* budget. So do you think they are going to find a way to cut more than $1 trillion in order to balance the annual budget and create a surplus? I think the current political environment makes it unlikely.

What do you think?

Prepare now.

Chapter 9

WHAT WILL AMERICA'S FINANCIAL DEMISE LOOK LIKE?

S top for a minute and take a look at reality. America is on an unsustainable fiscal course. The numbers prove it, the government reports proclaim it, but the majority of Americans are still ignoring the data.

- Deficits in thirty-six of the past forty years
- $17+ trillion in total debt (the debt has not *decreased* in fifty-six years)
- It took 233 years to reach $10 trillion in debt (1776 to 2009)
- According to projections, it will take only eight more years (2009 to 2017) to add another $10+ trillion in debt
- The negative power of compounding interest is working against us
- The Social Security Trust Fund is "funded" with $2.6 trillion in IOUs
- The U.S. monetary base increased 305 percent between September 10, 2008 and September 18, 2013

- U.S. currency is no longer backed by the gold standard
- The U.S. economy is primed for inflation
- Interest rates are being artificially suppressed by Federal Reserve
- We are purchasing a large portion of our own debt
- The GAO has repeatedly warned of a shrinking window of opportunity
- A balanced budget alone is not enough to solve the problem
- The only way to pay down the debt is to create a surplus in the budget
- It appears that Congress is unwilling to solve our fiscal problems

It looks like the perfect conditions for a massive economic storm. *What do you think?*

If you remove the political bias and simply look at the facts, it appears an economic storm is on the horizon and will lead to America's financial demise.

WHAT WOULD AMERICA'S FINANCIAL DEMISE LOOK LIKE?

- America would no longer be the most powerful nation in the world.
- America's demise would result in the creation of a new world order.
- America would certainly be forced to yield sovereignty to global institutions such as the International Monetary Fund. The "one world" government concept would be that much closer to reality.
- America would very likely be forced to dispose of the dollar and join with other nations in the creation of a global currency. One example is the European Union.
- America would lose her global military influence and power, because a bankrupt nation does not have the monetary resources to pay for a strong national defense.

- The American standard of living would decrease, as our nation would no longer be an economic powerhouse in the global economy.
- American funding for global missions would be dramatically reduced. (America presently sends/deploys more funds for mission support than any other nation.)
- Every aspect of America as we know it would decrease: education, social welfare, humanitarian aid, health services, military, homeland security, and support for global missions.

We definitely have enough valid reasons to begin preparing spiritually and financially for America's financial demise.

In the next chapter, we will shift our focus from the government to *you*. What do *you* need to be doing? How should *you* view this topic biblically? How do *you* prepare?

My advice is for you to take your time as you read and study the PREP Plan. Don't approach the next few chapters as something to read just once. Stop and think about what you're reading, let the material soak in, reread the chapters, internalize the plan, and talk about it with your family and friends.

View the next few chapters as your PREP manual.

Prepare now.

Can We Solve the Problem?
Four Big Ifs

Before I move forward, I must summarize where we are today.

Can we be certain that America's financial demise will happen?
Unless our nation changes course, the statistical probability of a collapse is high. We don't know exactly *how* it will happen, and we don't know exactly *when*, but we do know it *will happen* at some point in the future unless we change course.

Can we solve the problem? The answer is yes, but it will not be without some sacrifice. It will not be without pain. Every option must be on the table. I believe the solution will require a four-pronged approach: (1) cut spending; (2) create a fair tax code; (3) create a budget surplus and (4) grow the economy. We must stop taking dogmatic nonnegotiable political positions to please a political base or to win the next election. We must be able to openly discuss cutting spending in all areas (including Social Security and defense).

1. Cut Spending by Overhauling Social Security and Medicare

Making these two programs "means tested" would be a major step toward solving our fiscal problems. With means testing, benefits would be determined based on a combination of a person's annual income and personal assets. Anyone who has sufficient other income or assets (according to a standard the government would establish) would no longer be eligible to receive a monthly Social Security check. Take Microsoft founder Bill Gates, for example. With his billions of dollars in assets, does he really need to start receiving a Social Security check every month when he reaches retirement age?

With means testing, Social Security and Medicare would become social welfare programs—like food stamps, which are already means tested. A person who earns $100,000 a year, for example, is deemed to have sufficient "means," and thus does not qualify for food stamps. But a person earning $10,000 a year would qualify for food stamps.

Simply stated, in order to ensure the long-term sustainability of both Social Security and Medicare, we must remove from the rolls people who don't really need the benefits. I assume that some form of phaseout would be implemented, by which the benefits for people with sufficient means would gradually be reduced over several years.

I realize this is an unpopular solution for many people who have paid in to Social Security and Medicare their entire working lives, but we have reached the point where we have limited options. With too little revenue coming in, and too much in benefits going out, the system is simply unsustainable—and raising payroll taxes is not an adequate solution. It is time to face the facts and make the necessary changes. Until Congress decides to make systemic changes to these "entitlement" programs, our nation's fiscal problems will never be solved.

2. Create a fair federal tax code.

Presently, we have thousands of pages of complicated tax laws, and lobbyists fighting to protect their special interests. We need to create a tax code that isn't driven by or beholden to special interests and lobbyists, but is instead simple and fair to all Americans. We should consider flat-tax proposals as one option. Most flat-tax proposals allow for a minimum income threshold before someone must begin to pay taxes. Debating the pros and cons of a new tax code is not the purpose of this book. My point is simply that we have a broken tax code that needs to be fixed. Until Congress decides to create a new and fair tax code, we will remain on the same unsustainable course.

3. Create a budget surplus and begin paying down the federal debt.

A growing portion of the federal budget goes to pay the interest on the debt. Until we begin to pay down the debt, interest payments will continue to grow. In order to begin paying down the national debt, we must not only balance the budget; we must create a budget surplus. Is this possible? The answer is yes, if we make systemic changes to the programs mentioned above and overhaul our broken tax code.

4. Grow the economy.

Growing the economy would result in increased revenues to the federal government. However, growing the economy is only one facet of the solution. The GAO has documented the need for systemic changes, and we are past the point where only growing the economy can solve our fiscal problems.

"Absent structural reforms in these programs, budgetary flexibility will continue to shrink and eventually disappear. Our long-range budget simulations make it clear that the status quo is not sustainable. The numbers just do not add up. The fiscal gap is too great for any realistic expectations that the country can grow its way out of the problem."[38]

"This gap is too large to simply *grow out of the problem*. To be sure, additional economic growth would help the nation's financial condition and the ability to address the fiscal gap, but it will not eliminate the need for action."[39]

It will take a combination of spending cuts, tax code revisions, systemic changes to Social Security and Medicare, *and* economic growth to put us on a sustainable course.

Summary

The road back to fiscal sanity and away from America's financial demise rests on four big *"ifs"*: (1) *If* Congress is willing to make systemic changes in Social Security and Medicare; (2) *If* Congress is willing to make systemic changes to our tax code; (3) *If* Congress is willing to begin paying down the national debt; and (4) If we can grow the economy, America's financial demise can be avoided. *If not* . . . well, you already know what's going to happen.

What can we do?

As *American citizens*, we must let our voices be heard and demand that Congress make the necessary systemic changes—even if they are unpopular. As *Christian believers*, it is our duty that we must *pray*—consistently and continually—for our nation and our leaders. As *individuals*, we must PREPARE. Unless you are a member of Congress, you do not have the power to cast a vote for any of the systemic changes I listed above. However, you do have the power to vote and to control your personal finances. You can make the decision to pay down or pay off your personal debt. You can decide how much to give and how much to save. And can you decide—and commit yourself—to live within your means. And finally, you can make the decision to prepare as best you can for the coming economic storm.

Prepare now.

Chapter 10

IT'S NOW
ABOUT *YOU*

How many times have you said, or heard someone say, "We are mortgaging the financial future of our kids and grandkids!" The focus is always on the younger generations, implying that the problems will not occur until sometime in the distant future—not in our lifetimes.

But the timeline has changed.

The last seventy-nine years of overspending by Democrats and Republicans in Congress have set the stage for America's financial demise. Now, with the addition of unprecedented levels of government spending over the past few years, and the recent trillion-dollar deficits, the timeline for an economic crisis has shifted forward.

THE FUTURE IS NOW

The concern is no longer just for our children and grandchildren. The future we have mortgaged is now *our own* as well!

It doesn't matter whether you are twenty, forty, sixty, or eighty years old, the probability that you will be personally affected by the economic storm is very likely. Unless we change course soon, *you* will see America's financial demise *in your lifetime.*

THE TIMELINE CHANGED IN 2009	
Before 2009	2009 and Beyond
Concern for your children and grandchildren. They will be the ones who have to pay for our nation's mistakes.	The timeline has changed. It is now about you— and your children and grandchildren.

In the face of staggering annual deficits, a projected *doubling* of the national debt in eight short years, negative compounding interest, expansion of the monetary base, the Federal Reserve buying our own debt, artificially low interest rates . . . what can we as individuals do?

We can start by doing three things:

- face the facts
- pray for a miracle
- prepare for the most predictable economic storm in our nation's history.

In the next few chapters, I will teach you what I call the PREP Plan, a four-part response based on a biblical perspective and solid financial advice.

Here are the basic principles of the PREP Plan:

- *timeless*, meaning they will work during any economic season (economic prosperity, normal economic growth or global economic Armageddon).
- *applicable to anyone*, regardless of age, status, or financial condition
- *global*, meaning they will work in any country and any economy.

Take your time as you go through the next several chapters. Consider rereading each PREP chapter once or twice before moving on to the next.

My goal is not simply to rehash well-known financial principles, but to take a *fresh look* at what it means to prepare.

Prepare now.

PLAN

What do I need to do?

PREPARE

Chapter 11

THE PREP PLAN

As I have carefully documented in chapters 1–10, a major economic storm is coming. It could end up being a hurricane, or a tsunami. It doesn't matter if the economic storm arrives full force, or is weakened; either way, we need to be prepared and to help others prepare.

The wise see danger ahead and prepare; a fool ignores the facts and suffers the consequences.
—Proverbs 27:12

After examining the facts in the previous chapters, do you see economic danger ahead?

As I interact with people across the nation (and in other countries), I have found that most people have not examined the facts or put much thought into preparing for an economic storm. The most common solution we hear from our friends, or on infomercials, is this: buy *guns* and *gold*.

Is that the best we can do?

That might be *part* of your preparation, but it's surely not everything—and it isn't even where we need to start.

The soundest advice comes directly from God's Word, the

Bible, the best-selling book in the history of the world. Not from an infomercial.

I believe the best way to prepare is by following four timeless and tested principles—based on biblical counsel—that I've been teaching for more than twenty-five years. I'm convinced that this PREP Plan will work for any person, in any nation, in any economic scenario.

THE PREP PLAN OVERVIEW	
P	Prepare Spiritually
R	Reallocate Resources
E	Economize Lifestyle
P	Pay Off Debt

STOP. Take a minute right now to memorize the four aspects of the PREP Plan.

Once you have memorized it, teach it to your family, friends, and associates. Use the PREP Plan to spark a conversation about the coming storm. Give others a copy of this book and invite them to discuss it with you.

If you find yourself getting lost in the fog of dense economic reports and media hype and need a simple reminder about what you should be doing, remember P-R-E-P:

- **P**repare Spiritually
- **R**eallocate Resources
- **E**conomize Lifestyle
- **P**ay Off Debt

These four principles have worked in every economic season—from the Great Depression, beginning in 1929, through the prosperity years of the 1990s, and through the recent economic turmoil, right up to the present day. These four principles should become your north star. They're *simple, strategic,* and *practical.* They form the foundation on which everything taught in this book is built upon.

When friends or family have questions or concerns about the economy, you will be prepared to discuss your understanding of the problem and your plan of action. When the economic storm comes ashore, you will already have your resources strategically diversified. In other words, you will be prepared.

Those who were *spiritually prepared* before the Great Depression were able to live by faith (not fear) and encourage others during those dark economic years when unemployment was 25 percent or higher.

During the 1990s, when tech stocks and mutual funds offered astronomical returns, those who kept their *resources diversified* were able to avoid the temptations of greed and avoid catastrophic losses when the tech bubble burst in 2000.

Those who had an *economized lifestyle* before the crash in 1929 were in a better position to survive and thrive than those who were living beyond their means or those who had mortgaged their homes to put money in the booming stock market. During the prosperous 1990s, those who had an economized lifestyle were able to invest their surplus, greatly multiply resources, and live a lifestyle of generosity toward others.

During the 1930s, those who had paid-off debt or low debt were in the best position to survive the Great Depression. Those who had extra cash (because it wasn't needed for debt service) were in the best position to purchase real estate and stocks at fire-sale prices during the Depression. Not everyone lost money during the Depression. Some families actually became very wealthy because they were prepared. This is where planning and wisdom comes in.

There is nothing complicated about putting biblical principles into practice. You don't need a seminary degree or an MBA. A little common sense and discipline will serve you just fine.

Because the PREP Plan is based on biblical principles, you will be like the wise man in Matthew 7:24-27:

> *Therefore everyone who hears these words of Mine, and acts on them, may be compared to a wise man, who built his house upon the rock. And the rain descended, and the floods came, and the winds blew and burst against that house; and yet it did not fall, for it had been founded upon the rock. And everyone who hears these words of Mine, and does not act upon them, will be like a foolish man who built his house upon the sand. The rain descended, and the floods came, and the winds blew, and burst against that house and it fell, and great was its fall.*

Note that the rain descended, and the floods came, and the winds blew and burst against *both* houses. So, even being prepared does not mean that you will avoid being in the middle of the storm.

UNDERSTANDING THE PREP PLAN

The PREP Plan is *not* a checklist, to be completed one step at a time. Though the parts are presented in a certain order, you will put all four principles into practice *concurrently*.

- You will never stop preparing spiritually.
- You will never stop praying and asking God for wisdom about how to best reallocate your resources in this changing economy.
- You will continually evaluate how to economize your lifestyle and be a faithful steward.
- If you follow the plan, a day will come when you will be debt free, but you will still need to keep that area of your life in check and under control.

I understand that some families (especially single parents) need every dollar that comes in and will find it impossible to implement everything I teach in the PREP Plan. If this is true for you, don't be discouraged. Ask God to help you implement as many parts of the plan as possible. I know that you can implement the first, and most important, aspect taught in the next chapter: *prepare spiritually.* So start there and activate the other areas as resources become available.

In the next four chapters we will take a closer look at what it means to (1) prepare spiritually; (2) reallocate your resources; (3) economize your lifestyle; and (4) pay off your debt.

Prepare now.

Chapter 12

PREPARE SPIRITUALLY

I'm confident that, after reading the first half of this book, you would agree that we are approaching an economic crisis in our nation unless we change course soon. I'm even more confident that the number one question on your mind is the same one I hear from everyone who reads this book or attends one of my seminars: "How do I prepare financially?"

Am I right?

After listening to one of my presentations, a young couple asked me, "How can we best protect our $5,000 savings during an economic storm?" A few weeks later, a very successful businessman asked, "Ethan, what is the best strategic plan to protect my resources?" He was talking about millions of dollars, not thousands. It doesn't matter if you have nothing, thousands, millions, or billions; everyone is asking the same question.

For months, when I took my early-morning walk, I worked on how to best answer the #1 question.

But I was never completely satisfied with my answer.

Then one morning I realized that everyone, including me, was asking the wrong question.

The first and most important question is not, "How can I prepare financially?" but, "How can I prepare spiritually?"

We were all asking the wrong first question.

This is why Prepare Spiritually is the first thing we need to focus on as we implement the PREP Plan. One of the guiding principles in God's Word is that *the spiritual aspect must always precede the physical*. This principle is stated best in Matthew 6:33: "But seek first His kingdom and His righteousness; and all these things shall be added to you."

Joseph, who was beaten and sold into slavery by his brothers, had to understand the spiritual context before he could understand his physical hardships and his ultimate purpose in life (Genesis 45:5-8).

King Saul failed to understand that spiritual obedience is better than physical sacrifice (1 Samuel 15:22).

King Solomon teaches us in Proverbs 15:16: "Better a little with the fear of the Lord, than great treasure and turmoil with it."

Which is more important? To own the entire world (physical) or to know Christ (spiritual)? "For what will a man be profited, if he gains the whole world, and forfeits his soul?" (Matthew 16:26).

"He is before all things, and in Him all things hold together. He is also head of the body, the church; and He is the beginning, the firstborn from the dead; so that He Himself will come to have first place in everything" (Colossians 1:17-18).

See also: Proverbs 28:6; Matthew 6:19-20; 6:24; 2 Corinthians 8:1-5; Philippians 3:7-14; and 1 Timothy 6:6-10.

FOCUSED AND INTENTIONAL

As you begin to prepare for the coming economic storm, don't spend all your time and energy focusing on *financial* preparation. Start by preparing your life *spiritually*. Spiritual preparation is *not* something you'll "check off the list" as you move on to other aspects of your preparation. Spiritual preparation is the *foundation* for the other steps, and it is also an ongoing, daily, and lifelong process.

83

In order to prepare successfully, you must be *focused* and *intentional* about preparing spiritually, reallocating resources, economizing your lifestyle, and paying off debts. These steps will not just happen. You must *make* them happen. "Discipline yourself for the purpose of godliness" (1 Timothy 4:7).

Let me give you three examples of what it means to be *focused* and *intentional*:

1. *During my sophomore year in college, I began training months in advance to prepare for a summer in Quantico, Virginia, at a U.S. Marine Corps boot camp. I had signed up for a Marine officer's training program called Platoon Leaders Class (PLC), which operated during the summer months. As the summer approached, I got up early every morning to run, do push-ups, sit-ups and pull-ups. I knew that Marine boot camp was on the horizon, and I needed to be focused and intentional in my preparation.*

   I would have been a fool to arrive out of shape in Quantico. And, even having prepared, the training was rigorous and challenging. Though I never served full time with the Marines after college, I learned some important lessons at Quantico that prepared me for the rest of my life.

2. *For fifteen years, my family lived sixty miles from the Gulf of Mexico. During those years, numerous hurricanes came our way. Whenever a hurricane was in the forecast, we were always focused as we closed the shutters on our home, moved all the outdoor furniture into the garage, secured the wood pile, and purchased additional batteries, gas, water and food. We never ignored the warnings, and we were always focused and intentional in our preparation.*

3. *Years ago, my wife, Janet, committed herself to memorizing Scripture in order to have a closer walk with God*

(*Psalm 119*:10-16). To date, she has memorized fifteen books of the Bible and numerous other passages, such as the Sermon on the Mount (Matthew 5-7). In all, she has 140 chapters of God's Word stored in her heart, and she continues to add more every year.

How did Janet memorize 140 chapters of the Bible? Over the years, she has been *focused* and *intentional*. She will be the first to tell you that she doesn't have a photographic memory. She perseveres because of the joy it brings her.

The apostle Paul advises, "Run in such a way that you may win" (1 Corinthians 9:24). Focused and intentional.

About himself, Paul writes, "I run in such a way, as not without aim. . . . I discipline my body and make it my slave" (1 Corinthians 9:26-27). Focused and intentional.

"I press on toward the goal for the prize of the upward call of God in Christ Jesus" (Philippians 3:14). Focused and intentional.

"As you have received Christ Jesus the Lord, so walk in Him" (Colossians 2:6). Focused and intentional.

Think about Noah building the ark; Solomon building the Temple; and Nehemiah rebuilding the wall at Jerusalem. Focused and intentional.

I don't know of one person who has achieved great things (parenting, marriage, education, athletics, business, career, financial, spiritual) who has not been *focused* and *intentional*.

Use my PREP Plan to help you develop your own plan. Not everyone's plan will be exactly the same. The most important thing is that you *start* your *focused* and *intentional* spiritual preparation *today*.

WHAT DOES IT MEAN TO PREPARE SPIRITUALLY?

Whenever I think of how to respond biblically to an economic or personal crisis, I always think of Job. It's an amazing story of a man who trusted God through an economic storm and the loss of loved ones.

Job was one of the wealthiest men alive in his day. Job 1:3 says he was "the greatest of all the men of the east." But shortly after his story begins, Job loses everything—all his possessions and all his children. *Everything. Gone. Whoosh. Vanished.*

Job was at home when the reports began to arrive:

"The Sabeans attacked and stole all your oxen and donkeys."

"A great fire from heaven destroyed all your sheep."

"The Chaldeans raided the ranch, stole all your camels, and killed all your servants."

"A great wind blew down your eldest son's home and killed all your children."

And that's just chapter 1. As the story continues, Job encounters serious health problems and accusations from his wife and his three closest friends.

But now for the rest of the story . . .

Job was a man who feared God and turned away from evil (Job 1:1). He walked with God daily. And because Job was a godly man, he was able to say, after losing his family and all his possessions, "Naked I came from my mother's womb, and naked I shall return there. The Lord gave and the Lord has taken away. Blessed be the name of the Lord." (Job 1:21; see also 1 Timothy 6:7).

Then Job's wife comes to him and says, "Do you still hold fast your integrity? Curse God and die!" (Job 2:9). Obviously, she doesn't have the gift of encouragement! But how does Job respond? He says, "Shall we indeed accept good from God and not accept adversity?" (Job 2:10).

Job is one of our biblical models for how to prepare spiritually for any national, economic, or personal crisis. He is a hero of the faith. By studying the book of Job, we learn that he walked with God, trusted God's sovereignty, acknowledged that the Lord gives and takes away, and that we are to accept both goodness and adversity from our sovereign God.

HOW DO WE PREPARE SPIRITUALLY?

1. Begin with God

Our spiritual preparation always begins with God. The very first verse in the Bible says, "In the beginning God created the heavens and the earth" (Genesis 1:1).

Do you believe there is a God? There are only two possible answers: *yes* or *no*. A *maybe* is actually a *no*.

Do you believe that Jesus died to forgive your sins, and that He offers you eternal life?

> *"As many as received Him [Jesus], to them He gave the right to become children of God".*
> —John 1:12

Christianity is based on our having a relationship with Jesus Christ. Without a personal relationship with Him, you will not be able to understand and apply biblical principles.

> *The person without the Spirit does not accept the things that come from the Spirit of God but considers them foolishness, and cannot understand them because they are discerned only through the Spirit.*
> —1 Corinthians 2:14, NIV

If you are uncertain about your relationship with Jesus, or want to know how to establish a personal relationship with Him, search online for "Four Spiritual Laws," or go to www.cru.org/how-to-know-god/index.htm.

2. Focus on God's Word

To prepare yourself spiritually, I recommend that you become *focused* and *intentional* about reading, meditating on, and memorizing God's Word.

"Let the word of Christ richly dwell within you" (Colossians 3:16).

Whenever I'm asked how to prepare for the coming economic storm, I say, "Start by memorizing Proverbs 27:12: 'The wise see danger ahead and prepare; a fool ignores the facts and suffers the consequences.'"

Note the progression and key words in this verse.

The wise see danger (*face the facts/know the data*) ahead (*on the horizon*) and prepare (*become focused and intentional*). A fool, on the other hand, ignores the facts (*rejects the data, succumbs to cognitive dissonance*) and suffers the consequences (*pain and loss*).

Write Proverbs 27:12 on a 3x5 card and take it with you everywhere you go. Meditate on it, and memorize it. Store it in your heart. God will use this verse to continually remind you that the wise see danger ahead and prepare; a fool ignores the facts and suffers the consequences.

Over and over again in my life, I have seen how God uses Scripture I have stored in my heart to guide me when I find myself in the middle of a storm.

One of the literal storms in my life took place on August 29, 2005. You might remember it as Hurricane Katrina.

Words are totally insufficient to explain the experience and the destruction—the rolling dark clouds, the high pitched whistling wind, horizontal rain pounding against the doors and windows, the sound of glass breaking, explosive flashes of lightning that lit up the darkened rooms, the ground-shaking sound of thunder, static filled radio broadcasts, inoperable cell phones, spin-off tornados, the slow-motion crackling sound of trees breaking and falling onto and into our home, the rush of adrenaline, and the pounding of my heart. After the first tree fell and shook our home,

I can assure you we were on full alert. My wife and I spent five hours huddled in a small bathroom under the main stairs in our home.

The hurricane itself was intense enough, but I was not prepared for what I would find when I walked outside for the first time after the storm. What I saw will be etched in my mind forever.

There was destruction and chaos everywhere around me. Massive tall pine trees were inside of homes and crisscrossed on the ground like pick-up sticks. Eight of the eleven homes on our street had trees that were either *on* the home or *in* the home. I saw a pile of trees and limbs on our house that went from the ground to the second story roof.

The beautiful, massive, one-hundred-year-old oak tree in our yard was no longer standing. I could not walk more than a few feet without having to crawl over or under huge trees on the ground. My mind and heart were flooded with questions.

Do we have enough insurance?

What will be the financial consequences?

How long will it take to rebuild (knowing that thousands of other homes in our city needed to be rebuilt at the same time, and that our city has a limited number of carpenters.)

All these thoughts and unanswered questions were overwhelming.

As I stood in the middle of the destruction, the Lord brought to my mind numerous passages of Scripture that I had memorized in previous years:

The rain descended, and the floods came, and the winds blew, and burst against the house; and yet it did not fall, for it had been founded upon the rock.
—Matthew 7:25

The earth is the Lord's and all it contains, the world and those who dwell in it.
—Psalm 24:1

The Lord gave and the Lord has taken away. Blessed be the name of the Lord.
—Job 1:21

A biblical perspective was exactly what I needed as I stood in the middle of the destruction.

I have had other major storms in my life. I'm sure you have your own list. When the storms blow in our lives, we must respond biblically.

D. L. Moody (founder of Moody Bible Institute in Chicago) said, "Take those Christians who are rooted and grounded in the Word of God, and you will find they have great peace; but those who don't study their Bible, and don't know their Bible, are easily offended when some little trouble comes, or some little persecution, and their peace is all disturbed."[40]Moody continues, "Learn at least one verse of Scripture each day. Verses committed to memory will be wonderfully useful in your daily life and walk.[41]

You don't memorize God's Word just so you can check it off your list. You memorize God's Word so that it will penetrate deep into your heart, mind, and soul and affect how you live, think, and respond, whether in days of prosperity or in days of economic storm.

In the back of the book you will find recommended verses to meditate on and memorize. Use these verses to establish your theology of money and possessions. Write these verses out on 3x5 cards. Use whatever Bible translation you like best. Take the verses you are memorizing with you wherever you go and meditate on them during the day. I recommend you begin by memorizing Matthew 7:24-27.

Let me tell you about another helpful resource. In 2002, my wife, Janet, wrote a book on Scripture memorization: *His Word in My Heart: Memorizing Scripture for a Closer Walk with God* (Moody Publishers). She has recently completely revised and updated it. She also has a great website and an online community blog: www.janet-pope.org. Be sure to check it out.

3. Pray Consistently

In addition to knowing Christ and storing God's Word in your heart, you need to pray consistently. I can't emphasize this enough. If you want to be prepared for whatever life brings your way, you must make daily prayer a part of your life (if you haven't already). Find a time that works best for you, and *pray*. I've found that praying during an early morning walk works best for me. If I can't walk early in the morning for some reason (such as an early morning meeting, bad weather, or traveling), I'll walk later in the day, if at all possible.

Not only do we need to be intentional about our prayer life, we also need to pray continually throughout the day (2 Thessalonians 5:17). What does this look like in real life? Let me give you several examples. As you drive to a lunch appointment, pray for God to give you wisdom and discernment. Before you make an important phone call, pray before you call. When a friend tells you about a personal problem, silently pray and ask God to give you wisdom when you respond.

I use my morning walk to spend time with God—praying, memorizing Scripture, and processing life. I don't listen to the radio, music, sermons, or podcasts. It's just God and me. I love it. It's my favorite part of the day. Over the years, I have grown to treasure those early morning walks with God.

I encourage you to find an approach that works within your life and schedule. But do make it a priority and make time for it. You won't regret it. I can honestly say that my prayer life has never been more consistent, and fruitful, than over the past few years. Prayer is a significant part of our spiritual preparation for years of economic prosperity or economic storms.

I love to meditate on and pray about the wisdom in Psalm 1 and Matthew 7:24-27. Look in your Bible right now and read these passages. Better yet, memorize both of them—store God's truth in your heart. Pray that He will use His Word to keep you on the right path (Proverbs 3:6).

As I walk, I sometimes find myself praying James 1:5: "If any of you lacks wisdom, let him ask of God, who gives to all men generously and without reproach."

In the months and years to come, our greatest need will be wisdom. Not the shallow, surface type of wisdom (just buy gold and guns) that comes from the world, but wisdom that comes from God.

> *If the axe is dull and he does not sharpen its edge, then he must exert more strength. Wisdom has the advantage of giving success.*
> —Ecclesiastes 10:10

We will need wisdom in order to make sound financial decisions. We will need wisdom about where to live, how to best provide for and protect our families, how to best position ourselves for opportunities to serve others when the economic storm comes ashore. And we need wisdom about how to best encourage others to prepare.

Listed below are some of the things I'm praying about concerning *PREPARE*. I invite you to join with me:

- For wisdom and discernment on how best to prepare spiritually and financially
- For boldness to discuss *PREPARE* with others
- For clarity in communicating the problem, perspective, and plan
- For love and kindness as I speak to others
- For understanding as I study the problem
- For a sense of urgency
- For a clear biblical perspective
- For our president and his administration
- For members of Congress to act quickly
- For Christian and secular news outlets to communicate the truth

- For God to bring like-minded people into my life
- For churches to embrace the message of *PREPARE*
- That I will not lose heart and become discouraged
- That I will be prepared for the great opportunity for ministry
- That churches will be prepared for the opportunity for ministry
- For the ability to understand God's perspective on this issue
- To be salt and light in the world

4. Community: Start a *PREPARE* Small Group

The fourth aspect of spiritual preparation is to create and foster *community*. One good way is to start a small group. We all need to process this information with other people—with family, friends, and coworkers. If you're not already in a small group that meets on a regular basis, I encourage you to gather a group of four to twelve people to begin to pray about and discuss the issues in this book.

God does not want us to live in isolation. He wants us to live in community, where we can freely discuss important topics, such as *PREPARE*, and learn from one another.

> *Fools think their own way is right, but the wise listen to others.*
> —Proverbs 12:15, NLT

> *Plans go wrong for lack of advice; many advisers bring success.*
> —Proverbs 15:22, NLT

> *Iron sharpens iron, so one man sharpens another.*
> Proverbs 27:17

> *Two are better than one. . . . For if either of them falls, the one will lift up his companion. But woe to the one who falls when there is not another to lift him up.*
> —Ecclesiastes 4:9-10

If you are already in a small group, I recommend that your group study PREPARE together. If you're not already in a small group, start one in your home, at the office, or at church. Schedule a time to meet once a week to discuss the book, pray together, ask questions, learn from one another, and memorize God's Word.

The primary way for God's people to prepare, both spiritually and financially, is through discipleship—the method that Jesus clearly modeled and taught. He influenced the multitudes, but focused on twelve men.

Paul was a discipler of men and gives us his model in 2 Timothy 2:2: "The things which you have heard from me in the presence of many witnesses, these entrust to faithful men, who will be able to teach others also."

Our goal is to teach others a biblical perspective on this important topic.

Before you go on to the next chapter, make sure you fully understand how to prepare spiritually. Turn to God, study and memorize Scripture, pray, and get involved a small group. Discuss these things with your spouse, family, friends, neighbors, and coworkers.

THE PREP PLAN
Prepare Spiritually *Know Christ — Memorize Scripture —* *Pray — Community/Small Group*
Reallocate Resources
Economize Lifestyle
Pay Off Debt

In the next chapter, we will take a closer look at what it means to reallocate your resources. I think you will find my perspective biblical, practical, and refreshing.

Prepare now.

Chapter 13

REALLOCATE RESOURCES

Al·lo·cate – *to set apart for a specific purpose; to distribute in shares or according to a plan*
—Webster's New World Dictionary

THE PREP PLAN
Prepare Spiritually
Reallocate Resources
Economize Lifestyle
Pay Off Debt

In all seasons of life, but especially when preparing for an economic storm, we need to be confident we are evaluating and allocating our resources in alignment with God's Word and sound financial principles. *Now more than ever before.*

Two days after the Bear Stearns bailout in March 2008, I was a guest on a national radio program and said, "Everything is going to change. We are now living in a new economy." History has proven that I was right. We are living in a new and vastly different economy, with more government intervention, more debt, and more economic instability. This new economy calls for us to be good stewards (more so than ever), active in managing and overseeing our God-given resources.

Let's think about the word *reallocate* and how it relates to our resources.

When nations are at war, they *reallocate* soldiers and resources to strategic locations in order to win the war. When businesses implement their business plans, they continually evaluate profit and loss statements and *reallocate* resources to expand the most profitable areas. When a family's primary income producer loses his or her job, the family prioritizes where to *reallocate* savings in order to stretch the budget. When nations, businesses, churches, families, and individuals have strong evidence that an economic storm is on the horizon, they all need to *evaluate* and *reallocate* resources wherever necessary. Reallocating resources is an active, not a passive, process.

Another key concept in this chapter is *diversification*. When you hear the word *diversify*, it usually brings to mind your investment portfolio, right? What is the proper mix of cash, mutual funds, bonds, stocks, precious metals, real estate, and international funds?

In this chapter, I'm going to broaden the definition of what it means to diversify, or reallocate, *all* of your resources, *on earth and in heaven.* We're going to expand our thinking and approach the subject from a biblical perspective. *I trust you will find my explanation refreshing.*

In the table below, you see my big-picture framework for reallocating resources—and it's not your traditional view. As we'll see, each area of diversification serves a specific purpose, yet they all work together.

BIBLICAL DIVERSIFICATION OVERVIEW	
	INVESTMENTS
	EMERGENCY FUND
	SAVING
	GIVING

1. Giving as a Financial Priority

When we bring a biblical perspective to the topic of reallocating our resources, we begin with *giving* as the base or foundation. According to Scripture, giving is a no-risk, high return investment that yields *eternal* rewards. *How could we find anything better?*

Why is giving the base? Think of it this way: Even if you were to lose everything you owned in this world, everything that you had already invested in the kingdom of God (church, ministries, missions, helping the poor, widows and orphans) would not be lost. *Period.*

Jesus says, "Lay up for yourselves treasures in heaven, where neither moth nor rust destroys, and where thieves do not break in or steal" (Matthew 6:20).

Notice what Jesus is saying. What are we to "lay up"? *Treasures.* For whom? *For ourselves.* Where? *In heaven.* How long will these treasures last? *Forever.*

So, when we *invest* in God's kingdom by *giving* of our resources, we benefit *ourselves* by creating *eternal treasures.*

The apostle Paul teaches that we each have an account in heaven: "Not that I seek the gift itself, but I seek for the profit which *increases to your account*" (Philippians 4:17, italics added).

There is no question that *giving* is the context of this passage. Paul says that when you give, your account (in heaven) increases. Whose account? *Your account.* What happens when you give? *Your account increases.* Where is your account? *In heaven.* How long is the account open? *For eternity.*

In 1 Timothy 6:18-19, Paul writes, "Instruct them to do good, to be rich in good works, to be generous and ready to share, *storing up for themselves the treasure of a good foundation for the future*, so that they may take hold of that which is life indeed."

Again, what is the context? *Giving.* Who are they storing up for? *Themselves.* What are they storing up? *Treasures.* For when? *The future, in heaven.* For how long? *Eternity.*

And Paul, again, in 2 Corinthians 9:6: "He who sows sparingly will also reap sparingly, and he who sows bountifully will also reap bountifully."

What is the context? *Giving.* Is there a connection between what you give and what you reap? *Definitely.* Does the passage say when we will reap sparingly or bountifully? *No. Could be in this life, in heaven, or both.* But, we will reap what we sow.

Jesus says, "For what will a man be profited, if he gains the whole world, and forfeits his soul?" (Matthew 16:26). Jesus' words could not be any clearer. Investing a portion of your resources in things that will never fade away is far more important than investing your resources in things that will one day vanish.

Please do not misunderstand what I'm saying. I'm not talking about *giving to get* in this life. I'm not saying if you give God (or your church) $100 that you will receive $1,000 in the mail next week. But I am saying that whatever you give to God will pay *eternal rewards* that will never fade away.

Reallocation of resources:

- Eternal or temporal?
- Guaranteed or not guaranteed?
- Increases your account in heaven or increases your account on earth?

This is life-changing, radical, yet biblical thinking. What does it make you want to do? It makes me want to build my giving base and invest my resources in things that will last for eternity.

Paradoxical isn't it? When you *give*, in reality you *gain*. This is God's economy at its best. It's totally contrary to what the world teaches and offers. It's the last thing the world would think of doing, but the first thing God wants us to do.

It's your choice.

The best the world can offer you are luxury homes, fancy cars, beautiful clothes, jewelry, gourmet foods, exotic travel, and money in the bank—all of which may last until you die, but then they're gone. *Whoosh.*

God's economy offers you treasures in heaven that will last *forever* (see Matthew 6:19-24, 16:26, 19:16-26; Luke 12:16-33, 16:19-31; Philippians 3:7-14; 2 Timothy 4:5-8; Hebrews 11:1-39).

Biblically speaking, this is why *giving* is the *foundation* for reallocating our resources.

It is our first financial priority, and it is our best financial priority.

We read in Proverbs that giving is our first priority in allocating our resources during any economic season—prosperity or depression. The Bible does not place conditions on when we should give: We give during *any* economic season.

> *Honor the LORD with your wealth, with the firstfruits of all your crops; then your barns will be filled to overflowing and your vats will brim over with new wine.*
> Proverbs 3:9-10, NIV

Giving is what we should do *first*—not last—when we allocate our resources. This is what the Bible refers to as giving of our firstfruits. We're to give to God *first*, not after we've spent, saved, and invested. We don't give from what is left over at the end of the month.

The world teaches, "Pay yourself first." The Bible teaches to *give* first.

There is a time to save, invest, and buy homes and cars; but saving, investing, and buying homes and cars are not your first priority.

Giving is a continual thing. As we earn, we give a portion—throughout our lives.

And we should not limit our giving only to our income. We should be willing to give from our assets and investments as opportunities arise. Maybe your investment portfolio has grown to a thousand dollars, or a million or ten million or a billion dollars.

Whatever your level of resources, prayerfully consider deploying a portion of your resources for Kingdom purposes. During your lifetime, you should continually diversify/deploy/give a portion of your resources.

Build your base. Expand your base. Don't ignore your base.

Giving is your foundation, and your foundation needs to be strong. From an eternal perspective, the stronger and bigger your *giving base*, the better.

You are only responsible to give out of the resources you have been entrusted by God. If your annual income is $25,000, give proportionally. If your annual income is $10 million, give proportionally. A person who gives $200 out of $1,000 will reap more in eternal treasures than a person who gives $200 out of $1,000,000. For one person, a gift of $200 might be sacrificial; for someone else, $200 is nothing more than a token gift.

From everyone who has been given much, much will be required.
Luke 12:48

What is the context? Being a faithful steward and knowing that one day you will give an accounting of how you managed the resources God entrusted to you.

For we must all appear before the judgment seat of Christ, so that each one may be recompensed for his deeds in the body, according to what he has done, whether good or bad.
2 Corinthians 5:10

Each one of us will give an account of himself to God.
Romans 14:12

The more you process these biblical truths and let them fill your heart and soul and transform your mind (Romans 12:1-2), the more you will desire to give, build your base, and deploy your resources (see 1 Corinthians 3:1-15).

At this point, our biblical framework of diversification looks like this:

BIBLICAL DIVERSIFICATION OVERVIEW
GIVING *Foundation — First Priority — No Risk — Eternal*

2. Small Surplus Savings Account: 10 percent of your annual income

Once you have established *giving* as the base of your reallocation, and as a financial priority, next you will focus on *saving*. Once again, I'm going to break with tradition and teach that your next priority is not to create an emergency fund, but to create a *small savings account*. I like to call it a *small surplus*.

Your goal will be to establish a savings account or small surplus equal to at least 10 percent of your annual take-home pay. So, for example, if your annual income is $50,000, you need a small surplus of at least $5,000. If your annual take-home pay is $100,000, you would need $10,000. The larger your income, the larger the surplus savings account you will need.

What is the purpose of your savings/small surplus?

Your small surplus will help pay for unexpected expenses that come up along the way—such as a major car repair, appliance purchase, home repair, or unexpected trip. You should already be budgeting for such expenses, but your surplus account is money you can use when a budget category comes up short. (Coming up short in a budget category is not an *emergency* in my definition. That's why

I don't label the small surplus savings account as an emergency fund.)

Let me illustrate the difference between your small surplus savings and your emergency fund. You would use your small savings to cover expenses when your budget category comes up short, such as when you need to purchase new tires for your car, you need to replace the hot water heater in your home, or you have an unexpected airplane ticket to your parents' home. An emergency is when you (or your spouse) lose your job and you have less income (or no income) for several months, or when you have to pay a *significant* unexpected expense (such as a new roof, a new car, or the cost of a cross-country move because of a new job). From my perspective, the primary purpose of an emergency fund is to help cover living expenses (housing, transportation, food) in case of a loss of income or because of an economic storm.

If you don't have 10 percent of your annual income set aside in a small surplus savings account, you should see the red lights flashing:

 *WARNING!*  *WARNING!*  *WARNING!*

Immediately declare a moratorium on *all spending*, except for things like giving, your house payment, utilities, insurance, and groceries. If necessary, have a massive garage sale, find a second job, or sell something to generate the necessary funds. Work to fully fund your 10 percent savings/small surplus as soon as possible.

Until you have your 10 percent small surplus set aside, I would *not* recommend funding your 401(k), 403(b), IRA, or education fund. Furthermore, this is not the time to go on vacation, buy new clothes, eat out, expand your cell phone plan, try to wipe out your credit card debt, prepay your mortgage, or buy a new car. Focus on funding your small surplus account as soon of possible. Do not delay. Make it a priority.

Where do you keep your small surplus savings?

I recommend you keep your small surplus savings in an FDIC-insured money market account at a bank or investment company. A money market account is like a checking account, but it pays interest. Most money market accounts have a check-writing option, so you can access your money at any time by writing a check.

At this point, our biblical framework of reallocation looks like this:

BIBLICAL DIVERSIFICATION OVERVIEW
SMALL SURPLUS SAVINGS *Savings equal to 10% of annual salary* *(money market)*
GIVING *Foundation — First Priority — No Risk — Eternal*

3. Emergency Fund: 25 percent (up to 50 percent) of your annual income

Because we are preparing for a major economic storm, your next goal is to establish a fully funded emergency fund. (If you have credit card debt or consumer debt, you should pay off those obligations before funding your emergency savings. We'll discuss this in greater detail in chapter 15). The purpose of an emergency fund is to give you financial resources to handle a real emergency that might come your way during a personal or national economic storm: a decrease in salary; unemployment; or a family member or friend in need.

Your first goal is to establish an emergency fund equal to 25 percent (three months) of your annual salary. So if your salary is $50,000 your goal is to have $12,500 set aside. If your salary is $100,000, your goal is to have $25,000. I know that's a lot of money, but most real emergencies require a lot of money. (Trust me; an economic storm is a real emergency.) That is why we call it an emergency fund. Think about how much it would cost to pay your expenses for six months to a year if your income totally vanished. If that ever happens, you will be thankful you prepared.

Once your emergency fund equals 25 percent of your annual income, you have an important decision to make. Continue to save until your emergency fund equals 50 percent (six months) of your annual income or keep your emergency fund at 25 percent and begin to invest additional resources. *It's your decision.*

Saving vs. Trusting God

Some people might wonder, "Can I have savings and an emergency fund equal to 25 percent to 50 percent of my salary and still trust God?" The answer is yes.

> *The wise man saves for the future, but the fool spends everything he gets.*
> Proverbs 21:20, TLB

> *Go to the ant, O sluggard, observe her ways and be wise, which, having no chief, officer or ruler, prepares her food in the summer and gathers her provision in the harvest.*
> Proverbs 6:6-8

Which is wiser? Spending and consuming everything you earn, so you have no savings, or putting aside a small portion of your income each paycheck for future needs? If you have no savings and you have an unexpected bill, what are your options? Pull out the credit card or take out a loan. Either way, you go into debt, which leads to *financial and spiritual bondage.*

Where do you keep your emergency fund money? Because of the economic storm on the horizon, I recommend you keep a portion of your emergency fund in an FDIC-insured money market account, and the rest in American Silver Eagle dollar coins.[42]

Why Silver?

In my opinion, silver is a better purchase than gold for most people, for six primary reasons:

1. **More economical to purchase.** *For most families, it will be easier and more affordable to purchase a few American Silver Eagle coins each week or month, than it would be to purchase gold.*

2. **Easier to barter, if necessary.** *If a day ever comes when you need to barter for gasoline or food, American Silver Eagle dollars will most likely be easier currency to use than a gold coin.*

3. **Greater potential for profit.** *Silver, which currently sells for around $25 an ounce, has a greater potential to increase in value by ten times, than an ounce of gold does, which currently sells for around $1,500.*

4. **Purpose of purchase.** *At this point in our plan, our focus is on establishing an emergency fund. We're not thinking about investing at this point.*

5. **Vanishing value (purchasing power) of the U.S. dollar.** *The U.S. dollar has the potential to crash. If that ever happens, your paper dollars (in your wallet) and digital dollars (in your online bank account) will become worth less or even worthless. However, in my opinion, on that same day, your silver coins should escalate in value and purchasing power. Gold and silver will become the go-to currency in the world.*

6. **Gold is primarily for larger ($) investments.** *In my analysis, you will add gold as an option (in additional to silver) when you need to invest significantly larger amounts of money in precious metals.*

Why American Silver Eagles?

I like American Silver Eagles because they contain 1 oz. of silver. Older silver dollars (pre-1935) contain approximately 0.75 ounces of actual silver. And it costs more to purchase an older silver dollar compared to an American Silver Eagle, because the older coins sell at a premium, due to their numismatic value (that is, their value to coin collectors). Why pay a premium when your main interest is in the silver content?

Why not silver bars?

My research indicates that silver bars are much easier to counterfeit than silver coins. Silver bars are sold in 1 oz., 5 oz., 10 oz., 100 oz., and 1000 oz. bars. Unless you are a silver bar expert, it would be easier for someone to sell you a counterfeit silver bar than a counterfeit silver coin. I'm not saying you should never purchase silver bars, but understand the risk involved. (The same logic applies to gold bars.)

Where should you store your emergency fund American Silver Eagles?

You have four primary options.

> **1. Safe deposit box** - *One option is a safe deposit box at a local bank. Is it 100 percent risk free? No. Someone could break into your box and steal the contents, or a natural disaster could destroy the bank. Or, if U.S. banks fail, there might be a period of time when you will not have access to your safe deposit box. Plus, there's the potential for new government regulations that would require banks*

to report to the government any content removed from the safe deposit box. So, you would probably not want to store all your silver in a bank. Safe deposit boxes are very safe, but be aware of the potential negative aspects.

2. **Pay for storage away from your home** - *You can rent storage space at a local (non-bank) vault. I'm not going to give any names or recommendations. Just know that they are available. A quick search on the Internet should give you some good leads. Be sure to do your due diligence before you store your silver somewhere other than a bank.*

3. **Investment company storage** - *Some precious metal investment companies will sell you the silver and then store it for you in their vaults. It's not my favorite option, because of questions about ease of accessibility when you would need to draw on your resources, but it is an option. Once again, be sure to do your due diligence.*

4. **Store at home** - *I do not recommend that anyone store large amounts of silver at home—for obvious safety reasons. I don't recommend that you store silver in your freezer, old coffee cans, under your bed, or in a hole in your back yard. And, yes, some people actually do this.*

Balance between cash and Silver Eagles

How much of your emergency fund should be in American Silver Eagles and how much should be in cash (money market)?

Everyone's situation is different. Pray and ask God to give you wisdom on how much to keep in your money market account and how much to keep in American Silver Eagle coins. My purpose is not to give you specific financial advice. My purpose is to help you *prepare* for a coming economic crisis by establishing a sound plan that includes savings and an emergency fund.

```
┌─────────────────────────────────────────────┐
│         BIBLICAL DIVERSIFICATION OVERVIEW     │
├─────────────────────────────────────────────┤
│                                               │
├─────────────────────────────────────────────┤
│                EMERGENCY FUND                 │
│    Savings equal to 25% (to 50%) of annual salary │
│     (money market and American Silver Eagles) │
├─────────────────────────────────────────────┤
│             SMALL SURPLUS SAVINGS             │
│   Savings equal to 10% of annual salary (money market) │
├─────────────────────────────────────────────┤
│                   GIVING                      │
│   Foundation — First Priority — No Risk — Eternal │
└─────────────────────────────────────────────┘
```

4. Investments

I have been teaching financial seminars for more than twenty-five years, and someone will always ask, "*Where* should I invest?" My response, for the past twenty-five years, has always been, "Have you earned the right to invest?"

Let me explain my thinking.

Investing is not the *first* thing we do; it is one of the *last* things we do. According to the PREP Plan, we have three goals to accomplish before we have "earned the right" to invest: (1) *giving* as a priority; (2) a small surplus savings equal to 10 percent or more of annual income; (3) an emergency fund of 25 percent (up to 50 percent) of annual income. If, and only if, those three priorities are in place, then you have earned the right to invest.

What it means to diversify your invested assets.

Perhaps you've heard the old three-legged stool analogy, which has been around since at least the 1940s,[43] when it was used to illustrate how Social Security; private pensions; and life insurance would work together to provide a family with financial security. In the 1980s, the same three-legged stool idea was used to illustrate the importance of diversifying one's investment portfolio among stocks, bonds, and cash.

As the illustration goes, we need all three legs to have stability.

If one or two legs are damaged or broken, the stool becomes unstable.

But if instead we applied a biblical principle that has been around since the days of King Solomon, our "stool" would have seven or eight legs, and far more stability: *Divide your portion to seven, or even eight, for you do not know what misfortune may occur on the earth*" (Ecclesiastes 11:2).

What if for some reason two of the legs broke off or were damaged? You would still have five or six legs remaining and the stool would remain safe and secure.

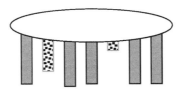

Think about investments in the same way. Build your investment portfolio with multiple legs. That way, if one, two, or even three of your investments experience a major loss, you will still have four, five, or six other legs supporting your investment portfolio.

The Future Is Uncertain

No one knows how the economic storms will come ashore. Will the pounding economic winds be inflation? Deflation? Debt default? Or will we see the U.S. dollar crash? *We simply don't know.* Be wary of anyone who tells you they know exactly what is going to happen and exactly when it is going to happen.

Remember the tech bubble in the late 1990s? (Actually, if you had money invested in tech stocks and mutual funds, you probably would like to forget it.) Many investors who reaped huge profits in the tech sector began selling other assets and transferring their money into technology stocks. Some investors ended up with between 50 percent and 100 percent of their investment portfolio in tech stocks. (After all, how could you not invest in a tech fund returning 70 percent or more annually?) When the tech stock bubble burst, many people lost 50 percent to 90 percent of their entire investment portfolios. Yes, 50 percent to 90 percent of their portfolio value vanished.

It reminds me of Proverbs 23:5: *"For wealth certainly makes itself wings, like an eagle that flies toward the heavens."* You can have $1 million in your portfolio today and nothing tomorrow. *Poof!*

For diversification to work, you must be diversified *across investment categories,* not simply invested in seven or eight funds within the same category. Back in the late 1990s, with all the hype about investing in tech stocks, some investors had *all seven legs* invested in some aspect of the technology sector—either in tech stocks or tech mutual funds.

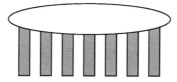

After the tech bubble burst, this is how things looked:

The best plan during the 1990s was to have your investments diversified, even if the tech stocks returned 70 percent annually. When the tech bubble burst, this is how your investment portfolio would have looked:

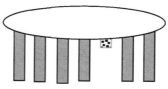

Your goal is to *reduce* your level of investment risk. Diversification helps to accomplish that.

Remember, "divide your portion to seven, or even to eight, for you do not know what misfortune may occur on the earth" (Ecclesiastes 11:2). This is great biblical and solid investment advice.

Before you invest in anything, I recommend that you ask the following seven questions:

SEVEN PRE-INVESTMENT QUESTIONS

Is this a get-rich-quick strategy or a hot tip you heard about from a friend?
If yes, avoid it!

Does your spouse understand and agree with the investment?
If no, don't do it.

Have you prayed and asked God for wisdom concerning this investment? If no, pray about it first.

Have you done your due diligence and researched the pros and cons?
If no, get to work and do your homework.

Do you and your spouse have peace about making this investment?
If no, don't do it.

Will this investment keep you fully diversified?
If no, don't do it.

Do you understand how this investment can make or lose money?
If no, don't do it.

Once you have established giving as your base, established your small surplus, and funded your emergency fund, how should you invest and allocate your resources?

I'm going to give you an overview of several major investment categories. The information that follows is to be viewed as general information, not specific investment advice. Every investment must be based on your specific goals, risk tolerance, investment knowledge, income, short-term needs, current portfolio, current economic factors, and your age.

Cash

History teaches that those who have cash during periods of economic crisis, such as the Great Depression, are able to purchase stocks, real estate and other assets at fire sale prices. Why? Because most people are so deeply in debt that foreclosures are rampant, real estate crashes, and the stock market is depressed. It becomes a supply and demand thing. Lots of people are selling and only a few people have the ability (cash) to buy. It becomes a buyer's market.

Several years ago, I started seeing articles stating that some hedge funds and private money managers were stocking up on cash. Why? They are waiting for a fire sale. Cash investments would include checking accounts, money market accounts, and certificates of deposit (CDs).

Unless our nation experiences hyperinflation, cash is good. If we do experience hyperinflation, the value of your cash can become worthless in a very short period of time. In that scenario, it is *not* good to have cash—another reason to be diversified.

Real Estate

Mark Twain reportedly said, "Buy land, they're not making it anymore."

Historically, real estate has been a good long-term investment. Examples of real estate investments include rental property (single residence, duplex, fourplex, apartments), commercial office space, commercial warehouse space, and farm land.

Yes, in recent years, real estate has taken a big hit in some cities (some property values were down as much as 50 percent and more), but it is showing signs of recovery in many major cities. So, let's all agree, real estate does not always go up in value.

If we have high inflation or hyperinflation, what do you think will happen to real estate values? One scenario is that real estate will *increase* in value. Inflation makes the value of a dollar less, so prices go up. A $100,000 home could become worth $1 million in a very short period of time. And if you had $100,000 in cash, it could be worth $10,000 or nothing.

But not everyone agrees that real estate will increase if we have high or hyperinflation. Some believe that if a major economic storm comes ashore, the value of real estate will greatly decrease because of rampant foreclosures—far more than we saw between 2008 and 2010. It is possible that 50 percent to 75 percent of homes with mortgages could go into foreclosure. In this scenario, homes and property could be selling at ten to twenty cents on the dollar. Also, real estate is not a liquid asset, meaning it might take you a while before you can sell the property if you need cash. And you never know when the government might step in and begin to regulate rental fees or increase property taxes—a*nother reason to be diversified.*

Even after evaluating all the pros and cons, I personally like real estate as an investment. But, like any investment, there is potential for substantial loss. Do your homework and be careful.

Gold and Silver

Why are people buying gold and silver? Most view precious metals as something that represents economic and global stability. If the dollar becomes worthless, gold and silver should not only retain their value, but may dramatically or exponentially increase in value. Gold and silver should have tremendous worth if you need to barter for goods or services during an economic storm. For thousands of years, gold and silver have been the *currency of the world.* When the world's fiat paper currencies (not backed by gold or silver) fail, what do you want to own? *Gold and silver.*

Many central banks have increased their gold holdings in recent years.[44] China appears to be quietly stockpiling large amounts of gold.[45] India's central bank is buying large quantities of gold.[46]

Russia has increased its gold reserves by 20 percent since September 2011.[47] According to a Bloomberg article, central banks own 18 percent of all the gold ever mined.[48] Do the world's central banks see an economic storm on the horizon and the eventual crash of the fiat U.S. dollar and other fiat world currencies? It appears they are planning for something to happen.

In our earlier discussion about how to establish an emergency fund, I recommended holding a portion of your emergency funds in American Silver Eagle coins. You might be wondering how those Silver Eagles fit into your investment plan. Let me explain.

First of all, your emergency fund is different from your investments. You should have an emergency fund in place before you even think about creating an investment account. The purpose of holding some of your emergency funds in silver and some in cash is to *diversify* your emergency fund as a hedge against inflation or the devaluation of the U.S. dollar. Further, American Silver Eagles are a liquid asset, meaning they can easily be converted to cash if you need to purchase something.

Gold can help give your family diversification in the area of precious metals. I personally prefer silver as the better investment (more affordable denominations and more potential for exponential growth in value), but gold may also be a good option, especially if you're dealing with hundreds of thousands or millions of dollars (as some investors are).

Silver and gold have many positive aspects as a long-term investment. However, in the short term, you might see your initial investment in precious metals decrease in value, as the markets are volatile. Let me repeat: The market for precious metals is volatile. There is great potential for substantial gains and substantial losses. Use gold and silver as a hedge against inflation and the dollar's demise.

The chart below shows what happened to the price of an ounce of gold when President Nixon officially removed the United States from the gold standard in 1971. Just imagine what this chart will look like if the U.S. dollar crashes.

Price of Gold per Ounce

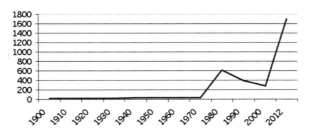

Stocks and Mutual Funds

Good mutual funds are always an investment option. If you are willing to invest the time and energy to research individual stocks, you may find some that are good investments—especially if you find a stock that is backed by a strong balance sheet.

If the government keeps pouring money into the economy by borrowing more money, we could see continued growth in the stock market for several more months or even years. Who knows, the Dow Jones could go beyond 20,000. Or it could drop to 2,000. That's why diversification across a number of different asset groups is a prudent and wise investment strategy.

Here's another question you might be asking: "If an economic storm is on the way, surely companies will lose money and stock prices will fall. So why should anyone invest in individual stocks or mutual funds?"

Part of what I've been saying is that no one knows exactly *when* the economic storm will come ashore. If the stock market produces a total return of more than 30 percent over the next three years, for example, wouldn't you like to have a part of that? Of course you would. The bedrock principle on which I'm building my investment portfolio is *diversification*. We don't put all our eggs in one basket. We allocate our resources and "divide our portion" according to the wisdom of Solomon.

KEY POINT: Let stocks and mutual funds be one aspect of your investment strategy, but *not* your *only* investment category. If the stock market continues to rise, a portion of your portfolio will increase. And if the stock market crashes, only a portion of your portfolio will decrease. Remember your seven-legged stool.

Oil and Gas

The world will always need energy; so it makes sense to consider having a portion of your investments in oil and gas. The most common way for someone to invest in oil and gas, or energy, would be to purchase what are called select oil and gas or energy mutual funds. Most mutual fund companies have *select* mutual funds that invest as much as 90 percent to 100 percent of their available resources in a specific investment category. A select energy mutual fund, for example, would be fully invested in energy companies (oil, natural gas), but would not have funds invested in computer, automobile, health care, or food companies. However, they would be diversified (investing in numerous companies) within a focused group (energy). You can find select mutual funds for just about any industry (including energy, health care, real estate, computers, automobiles, food, and transportation).

Bonds

When you invest in bonds, you are loaning your money to a business, municipality, or the federal government. In return, they promise to pay you a percentage of interest for the life of the loan. If your bonds are locked in at 5 percent and interest rates drop to 2 percent, the overall market value of your bonds (what someone is willing to pay if you want or need to sell your bonds) will increase; therefore, you make money. However, if you have bonds paying 5 percent and interest rates go to 12 percent, the overall market value of your bonds (what someone is willing to pay if you want or need to sell your bonds) will *decrease*, and you will lose money. So, when you purchase bonds, you have "interest rate risk," and you also take the risk that the lender will not be able to repay you when the bonds mature.

Personal Business

Whether it's a full-time job or something you do on the side, operating your own business may be a good investment strategy. Work on developing a skill or service that might be needed during an economic storm. If you have carpentry skills, for example, and lose your job selling cars, you could begin doing home repair work to earn income for your family. Even if you don't lose your regular job, a side job can be a good source of additional income for building your savings and emergency funds or helping you to pay off your debts.

I have always been interested in real estate. On occasion, I have purchased homes, rehabbed them, and resold them. I now have the skill set and experience to do more of that if necessary. So, I know what my backup, economic-storm job will be if necessary. What is your plan?

What skill(s) can you develop? Home repairs, car repairs, landscaping, tutoring, painting, computer repair, making clothes, tax preparation, bookkeeping . . . the list goes on. I believe that money invested in a personal business will be money well invested long-term. However, start small, develop your skill, and experience some success before you invest thousands of dollars into your business. For example, I purchased and rehabbed $40,000 homes before I started purchasing and rehabbing more-expensive homes.

How much should you invest in each area?

Everyone's situation is different. How you allocate your investments will depend on how much money you have to invest, opportunities that arise, and the need to diversify. Your investment table might have five legs, or ten legs. In my opinion, you should have a minimum of five areas of diversification (20 percent ± each), but no more than ten (10 percent ± each). Again, *that's just my opinion*. You might disagree. Making this decision is where prayer, wisdom, and seeking the advice of others become important.

Each year you might have some gainers and some losers. What you're trying to avoid is having all losers or having too many losses in any one category.

BIBLICAL DIVERSIFICATION OVERVIEW						
Cash/CD Money Market	Stock/ Mutual Funds	Bonds	Real Estate	Energy: Oil & Gas	Gold & Silver	Personal Business
INVESTMENTS *Examples above of diversification (not a complete list of options)*						
EMERGENCY FUND *Savings equal to 25% (to 50%) of annual salary (money market and American Silver Eagles)*						
SMALL SURPLUS SAVINGS *Savings equal to 10% of annual salary (money market)*						
GIVING *Foundation — First Priority — No Risk — Eternal*						

Just to be perfectly clear, the main point of this section is to establish the importance of *diversifying* your investments, not to give you specific investment advice. I do not know your personal circumstances, level of risk tolerance, or current and future financial needs. Therefore, the information provided in this book is not intended to give you specific investment advice, but to help you understand basic investment principles. Do not limit your investments only to the areas I have highlighted above. I believe these are good suggestions, but they're not your only options. Other areas include diamonds, jewelry, farm land, antiques, motor vehicles, farm animals, food, commodities . . . and the list goes on and on. *Do your homework* and *invest in things you understand.*

THE PREP PLAN
Prepare Spiritually *Know Christ — Memorize Scripture —* *Pray — Community/Small Group*
Reallocate Resources *Giving — Saving — Emergency Fund* *— Investments*
Economize Lifestyle
Pay Off Debt

Before you move on to the next chapter, let me encourage you to carefully review the content in this chapter—especially if the ideas and principles in this chapter are new to you. Don't be in a hurry to get through the rest of the chapters. Take as much time as necessary to process the information, evaluate your personal situation, and decide how you are going to reallocate your resources.

Is giving your foundation? Is laying up treasures in heaven a priority?

Do you have a small surplus savings account of 10 percent of your annual income?

Have you established an emergency fund of 25 percent (up to 50 percent) of your annual income?

Are your investments properly diversified?

Prepare now.

Chapter 14

ECONOMIZE LIFESTYLE

econ·o·mize: *to avoid waste or needless expenditure*
Webster's New World Dictionary

Here is my expanded definition of *economize*: The thoughtful, efficient, and intentional use of God-given money and resources; wisely and prudently making lifestyle decisions; having the ability to be thrifty without drawing attention to oneself.

Now for my best definition: "to think and live with simplicity."

I like that.

In our complex world, something just feels good about *simplicity*.

One of the lessons we can learn from history is that the less debt you have to service, during a financial crisis, and the fewer things you have to maintain, the more likely you are not only to survive, but to thrive—spiritually and financially.

How you approach this aspect of the PREP Plan depends on your stage in life.

If you are sixty years or older, you might want to consider how you can downsize and decrease your possessions. If you just graduated from college and you can pack everything you own into your car, you probably don't need to think about downsizing, but it's a good time to think and pray about what you really need, so that you don't start over-accumulating. Use common sense and factor in your personal circumstances (age, assets, debts, career, cost of living, family) as you read and apply this chapter.

If you're married, make sure that you and your spouse are unified in making lifestyle decisions.

What do I mean when I say to economize your lifestyle? Let me give you a few examples:

- Develop the attitude that less stuff is better. Every "more or less" decision should be made with prayer, intention, and unity (if you're married).

- If your closets, cabinets, drawers, and garage are all jam-packed with stuff, what can you do to downsize? Do you have things packed away in a storage unit? There are seasons in life when we might need temporary storage for furniture or personal items. But if you've been paying a monthly storage fee for years, you might want to consider whether you really need all that stuff.

- Sell any unnecessary assets you own, such as extra furniture, jewelry, or cars.

- Be intentional about lightening your load, not adding to it.

- Make wise spending decisions. Don't waste resources.

- Unless you are young and in the process of buying a house or a car, don't add more debt; instead, eliminate debt. (See my comments later in the chapter about buying a first home.)

- Refinance your home (more about this in next chapter)

- Pray about downsizing your home.

- Purchase a less expensive car. Sell a car.

- Live on a budget (I like to call it a Money MAP)*
- Look for ways to simplify your life, not make it more complex.

My focus in this chapter is more about your *attitude* and *mindset* about your possessions and lifestyle than it is about giving you a list of 101 ways to cut your expenses or telling you to get rid of stuff. If your perspective and attitude are right, the correct action steps will follow.

Over the years, I have tried to live my life by acknowledging four biblical truths:

- I am a soldier in the Lord's army; therefore, I must be ready to follow His commands. (See 2 Timothy 2:3-4.)
- I am a sojourner; therefore, I must travel light as I journey through life. (See Hebrews 11:13-16.)
- I am a steward; therefore, I need to faithfully manage the resources God has entrusted to me (giving, diversified resources, economized lifestyle, and paid down debt.) (See Luke 16:10-13.)
- I am a student; therefore, I must always be learning (like the sons of Issachar.) (See 1 Chronicles 12:32.)

A BIBLICAL PERSPECTIVE ON ECONOMIZING YOUR LIFESTYLE

Your lifestyle reveals your values

Our lifestyle is often a visible expression of what we *value* and what we *believe*. The Bible never addresses the specifics of homes or cars (size, price, zip code), but it does address issues of the heart (compassion, generosity, concern for others). Lifestyle is more about our hearts and our relationship with God than it is about whether we should drive a new or a used car.

---

* For more information on my book *Creating Your Personal Money MAP* and other resources, go to www.foundationsforliving.org.

Others are not the standard.

We don't base our lifestyle decisions on how other people live. They are not our standard. Others can have a positive or negative influence in our lives, and we can have a positive or negative influence on their lives. Focus more on how you are living your life, not on how others are living theirs.

Guard against this common default.

Without focus and intention, a common practice is to let our lifestyle increase with our income. As a friend once told me, "Expenses seek your level of income." We must guard against this trap. Instead, we should prayerfully and carefully determine how much is enough and live within our means.

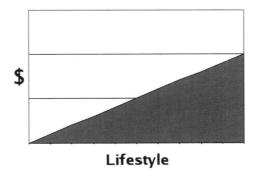

Lifestyle

If (or when) your income increases or you receive a significant windfall (inheritance, bonus, pay raise, sale of an investment), delay any lifestyle changes to give yourself time to process the change and pray. The greater the dollar amount, the more time you should take to pray and process.

> *He who loves money will not be satisfied with money, nor he who loves abundance with its income. This too is vanity. When good things increase, those who consume them increase.*
> Ecclesiastes 5:10-11

Understand the ways of the world

We must understand and acknowledge the materialistic philosophy of the world. Materialism is one of the weapons the enemy (Satan) will use to distract us, discourage us and depress us. We must resist him with the "shield of faith" (Ephesians 6:16). If we always want *more*, always buy *more*, and are never content with what we have, we will be distracted, discouraged, and depressed. We must guard against this (Matthew 13:22).

Distractions keep us from living intentional lives. Discouragement can come from being too focused on looking at and desiring what others have. Read the Ten Commandments (Exodus 20:1-17) to see how important this point is.

Don't rationalize your decisions or your behavior

The Bible is clear in some areas—such as don't lie or steal. But, in the gray areas, we can convince ourselves that just about anything we want to do is acceptable. As I said earlier, don't compare yourself to others or justify your own decisions based on what other people do. This includes, but isn't limited to homes, cars, clothes, hobbies, vacations, social events, education, careers, and raising kids.

Waste not, want not

Be careful not to waste your God-given resources by making wasteful and unnecessary purchases. One of the best ways to guard against an unnecessary purchase is to be sure that every purchase is accounted for in your annual budget.

There are no independent lifestyle decisions.

All decisions are interrelated. The size and price of the houses we purchase will affect how much money we have available for cars, clothing, and giving. Is the cost to live in your home limiting the funding of other needs? Is the cost to live in your home creating stress in your life or your marriage? The amount of debt we accumulate will affect the amount of discretionary money we have in the future. More debt to repay translates into less discretionary income. Have you ever stopped to consider that most families pay more in mortgage interest to the banker than they give to the kingdom of God each year?

Be transformed

Scripture commands us, "Do not be conformed to this world, but be transformed by the renewing of your mind, so that you may prove what the will of God is, that which is good and acceptable and perfect" (Romans 12:2). Don't let the world squeeze you into its mold. I can assure you, most people are not thinking about economizing their lifestyle, but expanding it.

Seek simplicity, not complexity

Move toward a life of simplicity and move away from a life of complexity. Over the past twenty-five years, I have counseled people and led seminars for thousands of singles and couples concerning financial issues. Some were in great shape financially, while others were in a financial crisis.

This is one of the big life lessons I have learned. The majority of those who came to me in the middle of a financial crisis were living very complex lives.

- They owned homes they could not afford, drove cars they could not afford, and wasted lots of money on gadgets, technology, clothes, travel, entertainment, and dining out.
- Ninety-nine percent were not living on a budget; they were living from paycheck to paycheck.
- Giving ranged from minimal to nothing.
- They had little or no savings.
- They had high debt payments, which translated into a high demand for more income to sustain their lifestyle.

- They were more concerned about what others thought of them (their image) than about having the conviction to live within their God-given means.
- Their attitudes were conformed to the standards of the world.
- The need for more income resulted in longer hours at work and less time at home.
- Kids were being neglected by their parents.
- Marriages were full of stress, frustration, frequent arguments, loss of love, isolation, and loneliness.
- They were experiencing a loss of joy in their lives.
- They often experienced a loss of sleep.

If you want to know what *complexity* will do to a marriage, just look at the list above. I have heard hundreds of couples' stories over the last twenty-five years. I have looked directly into their desperate eyes as they've told me their stories. I have seen too many tears and witnessed too many broken hearts. But, *I promise you*; it does not have to be that way.

I have also heard the stories of hundreds of couples who did it right and got on (or back on) the right path. They chose biblical simplicity:

- Living in housing they can afford, and driving cars that don't bankrupt their budget.
- Faithfully living on a budget.
- Living a lifestyle of generosity—deploying their resources, building their diversification base, and laying up treasure in heaven.
- Having money in savings and a fully funded emergency fund.
- Their lives are not overwhelming or complex, but enjoyable.
- They made a decision not to super-size every area of life,

but to economize their lives—and they are reaping the rewards.

- Not conformed to the world.
- Not focused on image.
- Less stress, less pressure, living within their means, and getting great sleep every night.
- Their low debt translates into a lower demand for income to sustain their lifestyle, and less time required at work each week.
- Able to spend time with their kids.
- Their marriages are fulfilling; love is growing.

Do you think this list is a fantasy? *Far from it.*

This is what couples can expect if they will follow biblical guidelines for living life and managing resources.

Are their marriages perfect? *Nope.*

Do they ever argue? *Of course.*

But the overall tone of their lives is different because they are seeking simplicity rather than living with complexity.

WHY ECONOMIZE?

Here are three primary reasons for living an economized lifestyle:

1. *To prepare for the most predictable economic storm in history.*

2. *To be a faithful steward as you manage resources.*

3. *To be prepared to help others when the economic storm comes ashore.*

As you prepare for the coming economic storm, think *simplicity of life.*

Economize your lifestyle.

Prepare now.

A Word to Young Couples
about Purchasing a Home

Because we don't know when the economic storm is going to come, and we need to live our lives with an eye to the future, I tell young couples or singles to go ahead and buy a home if that is part of their plan. But I also tell them to be sure they are making a wise purchase.

· Don't pay a premium price for a home. Live within your means and within your needs.

· Don't finance the home 100 percent; have a down payment to establish an equity base in the home.

· Don't qualify for a mortgage using two incomes (both husband and wife). Qualify with one income.

· Don't purchase a home unless you plan to live in it for at least three to five years.

· Have a specific plan to begin pre-paying your mortgage.

Chapter 15

PAY OFF DEBT

THE PREP PLAN	
P	Prepare Spiritually
R	Reallocate Resources
E	Economize Lifestyle
P	**Pay Off Debt**

In more than twenty-five years of financial ministry, I have seen that the best way for an individual or a couple to make it through a financial crisis (whether personal, national, or global) is to have low debt or no debt. Those who have high levels of debt and complex lives are the ones who suffer the most when the economic storm comes ashore. *Guaranteed.*

If you need a recent example, look what happened over the past few years (2008–2012). Home foreclosures were at an all-time high. Why? Because most families were living from paycheck to paycheck, had no small surplus savings, no fully funded emergency fund, and were using their home equity like an ATM machine to pay for restaurant meals, buy cars, clothes, gadgets, large screen televisions, and vacations. When they hit the first financial bump in the road, they lost their homes.

This is why your emergency fund needs to be at least 25 percent (and up to 50 percent) of your annual salary. Biblically speaking, this is not *hoarding*. Having a small surplus and a fully funded emergency fund is prudent and wise.

If you presently have debt, I recommend a four-step process to decrease your debt or to become debt free.

1. ELIMINATE ALL CREDIT CARD AND CONSUMER DEBT

First, your goal is to eliminate consumer debt—*permanently.*

After you have fully funded your small surplus savings account (10 percent of your annual income), but before you fund your emergency fund, you will begin to allocate *all of your available funds* toward wiping out high-interest consumer debt, such as all your credit card balances or consumer loans. The only time you will "save" during this phase of the plan will be to replenish funds you are forced to spend out of your small surplus.

Pay off smaller credit card balances first—no matter what the interest rate. In other words, if you have four credit cards with balances of $2,000; $3,000; $4,000; and $6,000, eliminate the smallest amounts first. Once you pay off your first credit card, add the money you were paying on the first card to your payment on the second card to accelerate paying off the second card. Once the second card is paid off, add everything you were paying on the first two cards to your payment on the third card to accelerate paying off the third card. Continue this process until all the cards are paid in full. Then cut up your cards and don't go back into debt.

Why pay the smallest balance first?

By paying off the smaller balances first, you gain *emotional momentum* for tackling the larger ones. Most of the time, emotional momentum is more important than maybe saving a few dollars by trying to pay off the high interest cards first. In fact, if you gain momentum by paying off the smaller balances first and accelerate your pay-offs on all your credit cards, you will actually save more money than if you start with the high-interest credit cards first, but eventually give up and never pay them off. *Building momentum* and *having a good attitude* are key components in paying off debts.

This is how it would work: Joe and Robin have four credit cards with a total credit card debt of $15,000. First, they should make a list of credit card balances with the smallest balance at the top of the list. Second, they should determine how much income they can free up in their budget to allocate toward additional debt repayment. By cutting back on cable, their cell phone plan, groceries, restaurant meals, gasoline, and clothing (as shown in the table below), they are able to allocate $300 per month to use toward accelerating the pay-off of credit card #1.

Credit Card	Minimum Payment Amount	Additional $ Added This Month	Total Dollars Paid
#1 - $2,000	$20	$300	$320
#2 - $3,000	$30	$0	$30
#3 - $4,000	$40	$0	$40
#4 - $6,000	$60	$0	$60
Totals	$150	$300	$450

As you can see, they continue to make the minimum payment each month on cards #2 ($30), #3 ($40), and #4 ($60), but they are now paying $320 per month on card #1. After they pay off credit card #1 (in just a few months), they will add their $320 payment each month to the minimum payment on credit card #2 ($30) and begin paying a total of $350 per month ($30 + $320 = $350) on card #2 while continuing to make the minimum payments on cards #3 ($40) and #4 ($60).

Credit Card	Minimum Payment Amount	Additional $ Added This Month	Total Dollars Paid
#1 - PAID	0	0	0
#2 - $3,000	$30	$320	$350
#3 - $4,000	$40	$0	$40
#4 - $6,000	$60	$0	$60
Totals	$130	$320	$450

After they pay off credit card #2, they add $350 per month to the minimum payment on credit card #3 ($40 + $350 = $390) while continuing to make the minimum payment ($60) on card #4.

Credit Card	Minimum Payment Amount	Additional $ Added This Month	Total Dollars Paid
#1 - PAID	0	0	0
#2 - PAID	0	0	0
#3 - $4,000	$40	$350	$390
#4 - $6,000	$60	$0	$60
Totals	$100	$350	$450

After a few more months, Joe and Robin can pay off credit card #3. Now they are able to add an additional $390 each month to the minimum payment for credit card #4 ($60) and begin sending the entire $450 per month to pay off credit card #4.

Credit Card	Minimum Payment Amount	Additional $ Added This Month	Total Dollars Paid
#1 - PAID	0	0	0
#2 - PAID	0	0	0
#3 - PAID	0	0	0
#4 - $6,000	$60	$390	$450
Totals	$60	$390	$450

With $450 now being paid each month on credit card #4, Joe and Robin will be able to pay it off in a little over a year.

KEY POINT: As you can tell from the illustration above, Joe and Robin kept the total amount they were paying on all their credit card debt at $450. Of course you can pay more than $450 each month if additional funds become available. Let's say you received a bonus or sold something and suddenly have an extra $2,000. What do you do with it? Add it to your next credit card payment!

If you are paying 18 percent or more on your credit cards, paying them off is one of the best things you can do financially. By paying off your 18 percent credit cards, it's like you are earning 18 percent on your money.

2. ELIMINATE CAR DEBT

After you pay off your consumer debt, I recommend you focus on paying off any auto loans you have. Building on the credit card example above, you should now take the $450 each month you were using to pay off credit card debt and use those funds to *accelerate* the pay-off on your car loans, to pay them off as quickly as possible.

Present Car Loan Balances	Monthly Payment	Additional $ Added This Month	Total Dollars Paid
#1 $5,000	$300	$450	$750
#2 $15,000	$300	$0	$300
Totals	$600	$450	$1050

By adding an additional $450 every month to your payment for car #1 ($300 + $450 = $750), it will be paid off in just a few months.

Present Car Loan Balances	Monthly Payment	Additional $ Added This Month	Total Dollars Paid
#1 PAID	0	0	0
#2 $15,000	$300	$750	$1050
Totals	$300	$750	$1050

Now you can allocate $1,050 every month ($300 + $750 = $1,050) toward paying off car #2. With this accelerated payment schedule, car #2 will be paid in full just over a year after you pay off car #1.

From this point forward, your goal is to *pay cash* for all future car purchases. You can do this by saving your previous regular car payments of $600 per month into a "cars for cash" savings account for future car purchases. Or you can allocate the full $1,050 into your "cars for cash" savings account. While you continue to drive the cars you have, you can accumulate enough funds to purchase your next car for cash.

3. ELIMINATE SCHOOL DEBT AND/OR MORTGAGE DEBT

The reason for paying off credit card debt first is that credit cards usually (not always) have a much higher interest rate and a lower principal amount than car loans, school loans, and home mortgages. So, for practical reasons, and to build momentum for getting completely out of debt, I recommend starting with credit card debt.

The same reasoning applies to why I recommend that car loans be paid off next. Though the principal amounts might be similar to a school loan, a car loan will most likely have a higher interest rate. So, it makes sense to pay off credit cards and car loans before trying to pay down school loans or a home mortgage.

In my PREPARE grid, if you don't have a home mortgage, of course you would focus on paying down your school loans next. And if you don't have school loans but have a mortgage, you would focus on paying down your home mortgage.

But if you have a mortgage *and* school loans, how do you decide which one to pay off next?

School debt is the most challenging debt for me to give "general" advice on. There is no common pattern for school loans. Some people graduate with little or no school debt, whereas for others, their school loans may exceed $100,000 and even $200,000+ (if you add in graduate school). In addition, some school loan interest rates are relatively low, while others are on the high side.

If the amount of your school loans is significantly lower than your mortgage, it makes sense to aggressively work toward eliminating your school loans first.

But if your school loans are close to or greater than your home mortgage, you'll have to make a decision: (a) focus on paying down your mortgage; (b) focus on paying down your school loans; or (c) focus on paying down both at the same time.

But here's something to keep in mind: Your home mortgage is a *secured loan* and your education loans are not—they're *unsecured*. In other words, your house serves as collateral for your home mortgage—so if you stop making payments, the lender can foreclose and you would have to move out of your house (unless you could sell it, of course). Most school loans, on the other hand, have no collateral—no underlying tangible asset—that can be foreclosed or repossessed. Therefore, if you have to choose between paying down your mortgage (which increases your equity in the property) and paying down your school loans, I would recommend placing the priority on paying down your mortgage to become 100 percent debt free as soon as possible.

That doesn't mean you won't eventually get around to paying down your school loans. I *do not* recommend that you default or walk away from your school loans. In my PREPARE grid, all loans will eventually be repaid. But if, due to the economy, I were forced to delay payment on my home loan or my school loans, I would have to delay payment on my school loans. If you presently have large school loans and a large home mortgage, you might consider selling your current home and moving to a less-expensive home in order to accelerate the debt repayment for both loans.

Not knowing your specific details, I'm not in a position to advise you about the order of paying off your school loans and home mortgage. This is where prayer and the wisdom and the counsel of trusted friends will help.

Pre-Paying Your Mortgage

Most lenders will allow you to pre-pay your mortgage each month by simply adding additional money to your payment. You can add any amount, and even change the amount each month if you want to. Check with your lender to find out exactly how they would like for you to prepay. For example, do they want you to send one check, or send your regular mortgage payment and enclose another check clearly marked for reduction of principal? It is very important that you ask your lender.

Numerous mortgage calculators are available free online. You can do a simple search to find them. Most of these calculators allow you to enter your exact data (loan amount, interest rate, months and how much you can prepay) and will tell you when your mortgage will be paid in full!

In the chart below, you will see various examples of how quickly a mortgage can be paid off, depending on the circumstances. The chart shows the results if you were to pre-pay beginning with your first payment. Of course, you can begin pre-paying at any time during the life of your mortgage—and the sooner the better.

Paying off your mortgage with one check

How many people who paid off their home mortgages and are debt-free have lost their homes to bank foreclosure? *None.* The lower your debt, the greater the probability that you will be able to survive an economic crisis—whether personal or national.

MORTGAGE PRE-PAYMENT CHART
ILLUSTRATING A 30-YEAR MORTGAGE @ 5% INTEREST

Mortgage $ Balance/ Regular Monthly Payment	Pre-Pay $50 Month Will be Debt Free in # Years	Pre-Pay $100 Month Will be Debt Free in # Years	Pre-Pay $250 Month Will be Debt Free in # Years	Pre-Pay $500 Month Will be Debt Free in # Years	Pre-Pay $1000 Month Will be Debt Free in # Months
$50,000 $268.41	21.3 years	16.75 years	10.3 years	6.4 years	3.67 years
$100,000 $536.82	24.83 years	21.33 years	15.7 years	10.3 years	6.4 years
$200,000 $1,073.64	27.2 years	24.8 years	19.9 years	15.2 years	10.3 years
$300,000 $1,610.46	28 years	26.3 years	22.3 years	18 years	13.1 years
$400,000 $2,147.29	28.5 years	27.2 years	23.8 years	19.9 years	15.17 years
$500,000 $2,684.11	28.8 years	27.7 years	24.9 years	21.3 years	16.8 years

If you have the financial resources to pay off your mortgage and become 100 percent debt free, why not do it? In over twenty-five years, I have not had one person tell me he regretted becoming 100 percent debt free. But countless people have told me that they regretted not paying off their home mortgage when they had the financial resources to do so.

Why? More than a few people have told me that, at one time, they had enough money invested in good mutual funds, stocks, and bonds to have paid off their mortgage, but when the market turned down, they lost 40 percent to 80 percent of their invested funds. If they had paid off their home mortgage with some of that money, at least now they would own their home free and clear. If we've learned nothing else from the tech stock boom and bust and the 2008–2009 decline in the markets, we've at least learned that investments are not guaranteed to be there in one, five, or ten years. We can lose money. That's always been true, of course, but now I think more people realize it in a tangible way. And yes, before you flood my e-mail inbox, I realize the stock market has recently rebounded and is charting new, historic highs in 2014. But just because it rebounded this time is no guarantee it will rebound in future years.

Before you pay off your mortgage, make sure you've already fully funded your savings and emergency funds. Also, be sure to think through what you'll need for buying your next car, college expenses, and other major expenses on the horizon.

"Losing" the mortgage interest write-off

A common objection to paying off a mortgage is this one: "*But I'll lose my interest tax deduction.*" Let's take a closer look at that.

Let's say you purchased a home and have a thirty-year mortgage at 5 percent. Over the course of the year, for purposes of this example, let's say you will pay a total of $1,000 in interest. Let's also assume you have enough resources to pay off the mortgage and your effective tax rate is 20 percent (taxes due ÷ total income = effective tax rate).

Option A: Keep the mortgage and take the interest deduction on Schedule A on your 1040 form. Remember, interest payments are *not* a tax credit (which would mean that your taxes are reduced by $1 for every $1 in interest you've paid); they're a deduction on Schedule A (which means you will receive a 20 percent reduction in your taxes for every $1,000 you pay in mortgage interest—so $200 on the $1,000 in interest you paid). When has it ever made financial sense to pay $1,000 in order to save $200? If you paid off your mortgage, yes, you would lose the write-off—but you also wouldn't be paying interest every month! The *net loss* to you in this transaction is $800. The banker is enjoying that $800, not you.

Option B: Pay off the mortgage and become debt free. Without a mortgage, you will not be sending the bank $1,000 in interest payments this year. By losing the mortgage interest tax deduction of $1,000 on Schedule A, you will have to send the federal government $200 more in taxes. The *net gain* to you in this transaction is $800. *You* are enjoying the $800, not the banker.

The "investment loss" misconception

Another common objection to paying off a mortgage is the "investment loss" misconception. During the 1990s I heard hundreds of times, "Why would I want to pay off a 7 percent mortgage if I can earn 30 to 70 percent annually in a tech mutual fund?" (Yes, you read that correctly. Some tech mutual funds earned in excess of 70 percent annually.) My response was simple: "Those returns are not guaranteed forever." Beginning in March 2000, many tech mutual fund investors lost anywhere from 25 percent to 90 percent of their portfolios. Money that could have been used to pay off a mortgage was lost when the tech stock bubble burst.

Again, no one has ever told me he regretted becoming 100 percent debt free. *Not one person.* Whenever people pay off their mortgage, they feel a great sense of freedom.

Refinancing your home

A few months ago, I received an e-mail from a woman named Ann, asking questions about refinancing her mortgage. Her current mortgage balance was $110,000 at 7.50 percent fixed with twenty-two years remaining. She was being offered a new fifteen-year mortgage at 3.75 percent fixed with total closing costs of about $1,500.

If she keeps her current mortgage, she will pay approximately $8,250 in interest this year ($110,000 x 7.50 percent = $8,250). It will actually be slightly less than $8,250 because the loan is being paid down each month and thus less interest will be due.

If she refinances her mortgage, she will pay approximately $4,125 in interest this year ($110,000 X 3.75 = $4,125). The savings will more than cover her closing costs (in less than five months), and she will be debt free seven years earlier. So, refinancing was a great decision for her.

How do I decide if I should refinance?

With a simple calculator, anyone can determine the answer to that question. Here is all you need to know:

- Current balance on your mortgage
- Current interest rate
- New interest rate
- Number of years remaining on current mortgage
- Number of years for new mortgage
- Total closing costs
- Estimated years you plan to live in the house

Here's an example:

Current balance on mortgage: $150,000
Current interest rate: 6.50 percent
New interest rate: 4.00 percent

Number of years remaining on current mortgage: 24
Number of years for new mortgage: 15
Total closing costs: $2,250
Estimated years you plan to live in the house: 5
Calculations:
*$150,000 x 6.50 percent = $9,750 (approximate interest to
   be paid in next 12 months)*
*$150,000 x 4.00 percent = $6,000 (approximate interest to
   be paid in next 12 months)*
$9,750 – $6,000 = $3,750 = $312.50 per month in savings
*Closing cost of $2,250 divided by $312.50 = 7.2 months to
   break even.*

If you plan to live in the house for more than eight months, it makes financial sense to refinance your mortgage. If you have a home mortgage, do some quick calculations to see if refinancing makes financial sense for you.

Avoid the #1 refinancing mistake

The number one mistake people make when refinancing is to swap into a new thirty-year mortgage. When you refinance, the goal is to *shorten* the length of your mortgage, not increase it.

Your goal is *not* to decrease your monthly payment. If you can eliminate seven years of mortgage payments by lowering your interest rate, while keeping your monthly payment the same, you will save thousands of dollars over the life of the loan. If your mortgage payment is $1,000 a month and you eliminate seven years (eighty-four monthly payments), that equals *$84,000* that will *not* be coming out of your checking account.

4. EVALUATE YOUR INVESTMENT OR BUSINESS DEBT

Based on what appears to be on the economic horizon, now is also a great time to evaluate any investment or business debt you have. I recently became familiar with an individual who had accumulated millions of dollars in real estate debt. Rental vacancies were higher than normal and he was beginning to lose sleep at night. So he put together a plan to begin selling properties and was able to become debt-free in three years.

Here's the question he asked himself: "Is it better to own 125 rental units, work seven days a week, and lose sleep at night, or to own twenty-five rental units debt-free, and have a life?" He decided he preferred the latter option.

You might disagree, but that's your decision, your life, your path, your family.

My PREPARE Plan focuses on sound financial principles that work in every kind of economic condition. That's why I recommend that you process decisions like these through the PREPARE grid.

When the economic storm comes ashore, most (but not all) businesses will likely see a dramatic decrease in business activity. Why? Very few people will be spending money. So, the less business debt you have, the better.

Let's use a rental property business as an example. If every rental property you own has a high debt-to-market-value ratio, you could find yourself in a severe financial crisis when the economic storm comes ashore. You'll still have to make your mortgage payments even if the properties are now vacant (or when tenants cannot pay). Your rental properties could end up in foreclosure. On the other hand, if your debt service is low, or if you have no debt on the properties, you will be in a better position to survive an economic storm.

As a landlord with low or no debt, you will be in the best position to offer your rental properties below market value and potentially have 100 percent occupancy. Landlords with a lot of debt to service will not be able to lower their rental rates to compete, and thus may have higher vacancy rates. But if your cash flow is already tight, and you're living on the edge, any financial bump in the road could bankrupt you.

Here's my point: *Be sure that you are building as much financial margin as possible into your business.* The more debt you have, the greater the need for a fully funded emergency fund. Do not try to run your business without an ample cash-flow margin and ample cash reserves.

Is it wrong to have debt? God's Word does not prohibit the use of debt, but it often warns us about the excessive use of debt.

SET A GOAL: BECOME DEBT FREE!

Everyone should have a goal to become 100 percent debt-free. It must become a priority in your life. If you never set a goal, it will never become a reality. Becoming debt free includes credit cards, cars, school loans, mortgages, and all business or investment debt.

Simply put, paying down your debt and becoming debt-free will help you prepare for the coming economic storm.

Three Good Stewardship Practices

1. Always pay your credit card bills in full every month.
2. Avoid using debt for consumer purchases (food, clothes, vacations, car repairs).
3. Work toward a goal of becoming 100 percent debt-free.

At the end of this chapter, you will find a summary chart of the PREP Plan. But the PREP Plan will only be helpful if you begin to put the principles into practice. Remember . . .

- The PREP Plan is *not* a checklist, where you do one thing, check if off the list, and move to the next thing on the list.
- You will put all four of these principles into practice concurrently.

- You will never stop preparing spiritually.
- You will never stop praying and asking God for wisdom about how to best diversify your resources in an ever-changing economy.
- You will continually evaluate how you can economize your lifestyle and be a faithful steward.
- When you accomplish your goal of becoming debt-free, you will still need to keep that area of your life in check and under control.

The PREP Plan requires action.

Prepare now.

PREP PLAN SUMMARY

Prepare Spiritually

Spiritual preparation is an ongoing priority.

· Begin with God (acknowledge His existence and sovereignty)

· Read, meditate on, and memorize God's Word

· Pray and ask God for PREP wisdom for the coming economic storm

· Community: establish a small group and study *PREPARE* together

Reallocate Resources

Diversification is an ongoing priority.

· Giving is your #1 reallocation of resources—build/expand your base

· Small Surplus Savings: Accumulate a fund equal to 10% of your annual income

· Emergency Fund: Accumulate a fund equal to 25% (to 50%) of your annual income

· Diversify Investments: 5 to 10 areas of diversification

Economize Lifestyle

A lifestyle of simplicity is an ongoing priority.

· Think and live with simplicity

· Guard against increasing your lifestyle as you increase your income

Pay Off Debt

Eliminating debt and remaining debt free are ongoing priorities.

· Eliminate all credit card and consumer debt—permanently

· Eliminate all car debt—permanently

· Eliminate school loans—permanently

· Eliminate mortgage debt—permanently

· Evaluate/eliminate business debt—permanently

· Pursue a goal to become 100% debt free

PERSPECTIVE

How should I frame this topic,
biblically and practically?

Chapter 16

WHAT IS A BIBLICAL PERSPECTIVE?

What is the PREP biblical grid? Knowing biblical truth is how we begin to understand and frame events such as life and death; prosperity and poverty; economic expansion and recession, success and failure; and yes, even nations rising and falling.

Without knowing and understanding biblical truth we open the door to placing our trust and hope in unworthy objects or people; we open the door for unbiblical thinking; unbiblical objectives, and unbiblical expectations.

See to it that no one takes you captive through philosophy and empty deception, according to the tradition of men, according to the elementary principles of the world, rather than according to Christ.

Colossians 2:8

SEVEN PRINCIPLES OF BIBLICAL ECONOMICS

Here are seven biblical economic principles that are true in times of prosperity and times of scarcity and depression:

1. God has not promised perpetual prosperity to any person or nation.

Nowhere in Scripture do we find God promising perpetual prosperity to any person or nation. God did say he would bless a person (example: Abraham in Genesis 12:1-3) and He did offer blessings to a nation (example: Israel in Deuteronomy 8 and 28). Thinking that America will have perpetual prosperity is comparable to thinking that we will never die. We know neither one is true.

2. We cannot predict when economic hard times might come.

No one knows the future but God. But just because we don't know exactly what is going to happen, or when it might happen, does not mean we should ignore the data.

> *The wise see danger ahead and prepare; a fool ignores the facts and suffers the consequences.*
> Proverbs 27:12

> *People can never predict when hard times might come. Like fish in a net or birds in a trap, people are caught by sudden tragedy.*
> Ecclesiastes 9:12, N L T

3. Accept seasons of economic prosperity and economic downturn as from God.

We are to be faithful stewards of God's resources in every season.

> *Enjoy prosperity while you can, but when hard times strike, realize that both come from God.*
> Ecclesiastes 7:14, N L T

> *The Lord gave and the Lord has taken away. Blessed be the name of the Lord.*
> Job 1:21

Shall we indeed accept good from God and not accept adversity?

Job 2:10

Though the fig tree should not blossom, and there be no fruit on the vines,

Though the yield of the olive should fail, and the fields produce no food,

Though the flock should be cut off from the fold, and there be no cattle in the stalls,

Yet I will exult in the Lord, I will rejoice in the God of my salvation.

Habakkuk 3:17-18

4. Understand the Joseph Principle.

If the data reveals that an economic storm is on the horizon, we should prepare. We should set aside a portion of our resources during years of prosperity that can be used during years of famine.

Let them gather all the food of these good years that are coming, and store up the grain for food in the cities under Pharaoh's authority, and let them guard it. Let the food become as a reserve for the land for the seven years of famine which will occur in the land of Egypt.

Genesis 41:35-36

Go to the ant, O sluggard, observe her ways and be wise, which, having no chief, officer or ruler, prepares her food in the summer and gathers her provision in the harvest.

Proverbs 6:6-8

The wise man saves for the future, but the foolish man spends whatever he gets.

Proverbs 21:20, TLB

5. God's people are not exempt from suffering.

Flip through the pages of the Bible from Genesis to Revelation and you will see account after account of people suffering because of the sins and mistakes of others. (Joseph, Job, David, Jeremiah, and Paul, just to list a few.) *It is no different today.*

It's naïve to think we can create a plan to completely avoid the consequences of decades of mistakes by our government. When the economic storm comes ashore, everyone will suffer to some extent. So don't put your hope in avoiding suffering; put your hope and trust in God.

6. Be anxious for nothing and pray about everything.

Be anxious for nothing, but in everything by prayer and supplication with thanksgiving let your requests be made known to God. And the peace of God, which surpasses all comprehension, shall guard your heart and your minds in Christ Jesus.

Philippians 4:6-7

God's word commands us to be anxious for nothing. What is nothing? No thing. And that means economic storms. But in everything, we are to pray. And that definitely includes economic storms.

7. God blesses and judges nations.

He decided beforehand when they should rise and fall, and he determined their boundaries.

Acts 17:26, NLT

How long will God allow us to continue on our current path before He decides it is time to judge America or renew her economic prosperity?

I think we're about to find out.

Prepare now.

Chapter 17

TWO GREAT OPPORTUNITIES

Conduct yourselves with wisdom toward outsiders,
making the most of the opportunity.
Colossians 4:5

When the economic storm strikes, those who are not prepared spiritually and financially may experience disaster. But some people will experience a spiritual and financial blessing—those who are prepared. *Which one will you be?*

OPPORTUNITY #1: SPIRITUAL OPPORTUNITY

Several months ago, I was sitting in the office of a close friend. *It was a day I will never forget.*

After catching up on family, we began talking about the book I published in 2010, *America's Financial Demise*. I gave him a progress report on my research and writing for *PREPARE*.

I said that when the economic storms come ashore, we are going to see the greatest opportunity for ministry in the history or our nation—but right now it seems that families, churches, and ministries are indifferent and apathetic. If our opportunity were to happen today, we would miss it. We would completely miss the spiritual harvest.

My friend leaned forward, and with great passion said, "Not everyone is ignoring the data. Some are actually preparing."

I said, "Tell me more."

"Ethan, one of my friends is in a leadership position with the Mormon Church," he said. "He explained that the Mormon Church is taking serious the coming economic storm and they are warehousing goods in different regions across the nation. When the economic storm arrives, they will open up their warehouses to the helpless and hurting and say, 'We welcome you, come. Come and join our family and the Mormon Church.' Then he told me that he has actually been inside one of their regional warehouses."

I sat there *speechless*. It was one of those sobering moments I will never forget.

My heart and mind were flooded with various thoughts and emotions. I was deeply saddened that individuals and churches all across America continue to ignore the data and warnings, but I was also *motivated* more than ever to *do* something—*to get out there and make a difference*—to help families prepare spiritually and financially.

When the economic storm comes, who is going to reap the spiritual harvest? *The ones who are prepared.*

You might be asking, "Why isn't my church preparing?"

Let's not be too quick to place the blame on someone else. The more important question to ask yourself is this: "What am *I* doing to prepare personally, prepare my family, my church, my neighborhood, my city, my state and my nation?"

The responsibility begins with you and me. Let's all become agents of change.

What are you doing to bring the coming storm to the attention of your family, friends, and church? You might be welcomed, rejected, or even labeled a doomsday prophet. If they disagree, respond with love, kindness, and grace—but keep asking them why they disagree. Talk facts and not opinions.

It's easy to sit on the couch and grumble about what everyone else should be doing. *But, what are* you *doing?*

How many people are you going to tap on the shoulder this week?

How are you preparing for the greatest ministry opportunity we may ever have?

While many (but not all) American churches and ministries are ignoring the facts, we must demonstrate to those around us what it means to trust God and prepare at the same time—to put biblical principles into practice (Matthew 7:24-27).

The prophet Micah declares: "What does the Lord require of you, but to do justice, to love kindness, and to walk humbly with your God? (Micah 6:8).

Do justice, love kindness, and walk humbly with your God. *I really like that.*

Blessed is the man who exalts the Lord even when the fields produce no food, and who isn't prideful when the crops are plentiful (Habakkuk 3:17-19; Jeremiah 9:23-24). It will be men and women who know how to live in prosperity and know how to live during years of drought who will be blessed.

Like the sons of Issachar (1 Chronicles 12:32) we need to understand the times in which we live, put our financial houses in order, help others prepare, and live with a sense of purpose and mission like never before.

> *So be careful how you live. Don't live like fools, but like those who are wise. Make the most of every opportunity in these evil days. Don't act thoughtlessly, but understand what the Lord wants you to do.*
> Ephesians 5:15-17

As I said earlier in the book, it is by God's sovereignty that you were ordained to live during this era (Psalm 139:16). Just like Joseph

(Genesis 45:4-8); Nehemiah (Nehemiah 2:17); Esther (Esther 4:14); and Jeremiah (Jeremiah 1:5) had specific assignments, God has specific assignments for you during these times—assignments that involve the advancement of His kingdom.

Don't just sit at home watching movies or sleeping, find your assignment and serve with excellence.

What is the great opportunity?

- For you to be prepared spiritually and help others do the same.
- For you to be prepared financially and help others do the same.
- For you to walk with God and model faithfulness in days of prosperity or famine.
- For you to be prepared for another great spiritual awakening.
- For you to make a difference in the world.
- For you to be prepared to have an eternal impact on those around you.
- For you to be right in the middle of what God is doing in the world.

When the economic storm comes and millions of people are helpless and hopeless, who will be prepared with spiritual and physical resources?

You?

Your church?

During the economic storm, the "fields will be white for harvest," but will we be spiritually and financially prepared to bring in the great harvest?

OPPORTUNITY #2: FINANCIAL OPPORTUNITY

For those who are prepared financially, opportunity awaits. It has been said that more people became millionaires during the Great Depression than in any other time in history. It would be hard to prove that statement, but we do know that a multitude of million-aires were created. Why? Because they diversified their resources, economized their lifestyle, and had low or no debt, and thus were in a financial position to take advantage of an economic opportunity. They were able to purchase large amounts of real estate, bankrupt businesses, and stocks with pennies on the dollar. Years later, when the economy recovered, great financial wealth was created.

It is not a complicated formula.

If you carefully read and apply *PREPARE*, I believe you will have the *potential* to not only survive the coming economic storm, but to actually create wealth, live a lifestyle of generosity, and be a beacon of light shining in a dark world.

Spiritual and financial opportunity are on the horizon.

Prepare now.

Chapter 18

TWO QUESTIONS

As I write the final chapters of *PREPARE*, my heart and mind are flooded with powerful emotions, convictions, passion, and a great sense of urgency that we must get this message out. Some days I feel helpless. Today, as I write this, I believe *we* can make a difference.

Think of how you can make a difference in terms of spiritual preparation, financial preparation, and changing our economic trajectory.

You've read the book, you've evaluated the data, you know the biblical perspective, and you have been given a PREP Plan.

Now it's decision time.

Can I count you in?

Here are two questions you need to answer:

- *Are you going to prepare?*
- *Are you going to help others prepare?*

The mother of all economic storms is heading our way, yet most Americans are clueless. They are simply ignoring the news and data concerning the coming economic crisis.

I've often reflected on my experience during that early morning flight; the three scenarios that unfolded following the captain's announcement, and how these compare to the coming global economic crisis:

- some people are distracted and disengaged
- some people are asleep
- others (like me) are on full alert

Disengaged, asleep, or *alert*? Which term describes you?

When the economic crisis comes, billions of people around the world will be affected. Why? As never before, the economies of most nations are linked to one other. As America goes economically, so goes the world. It would be a domino effect. At this point in history, America is the first domino and most powerful economic domino. If America falls, all the other dominos (nations) will be affected in some way. So, this is not just a warning for America; it's a global economic warning—for people living in every nation.

It is my hope that, with a genuine sense of urgency, and *while you still have time*, you will grasp the opportunity to prepare spiritually, prepare financially, change the course of our great nation, help others prepare, and prepare to help bring in the spiritual harvest.

We don't know if we have days, months, or years. Remember how fast the crisis came upon our nation in mid-September 2009? Within hours, we were facing a global economic crisis.

By the way, we don't have to wait for an economic storm before we begin the harvest; there is plenty of spiritual harvesting we can do today.

Surprise will not be a word anyone will use when the coming economic crisis arrives. We have known it was coming for years.

There will be no excuses this time around—only regrets if you have not prepared.

Let's begin with you and me and enlarge the circle one person at a time.

Prepare now.

PEOPLE

How do I stay connected and informed?

Chapter 19

JOIN OUR ONLINE COMMUNITY

www.PrepPlan.org

This book is only the beginning of the conversation.

Do you want to know more?

Do you want to join the conversation?

- Blog
- Facebook
- Twitter
- Charts
- Small Groups
- Invite Ethan to Speak

PREPARE
QUICK REFERENCE GUIDE

A: **Why Prepare Chart**

B: **Facts and Figures**

C: **Talking Points**

D: **Index of Charts, Lists, Definitions, and Websites**

E: **Quotes**

F: **Scriptures to Study and Memorize**

WHY PREPARE?

· You need to understand the problem

· You need to understand the biblical perspective

· You need a plan

· You need to inform other people

PROBLEM	PERSPECTIVE
UNSUSTAINABLE	*BIBLICAL*
The United States is on an unsustainable fiscal course and heading for bankruptcy.	What does God's Word say about economics, eternity, nations, and our individual responsibility?

PLAN	PEOPLE
PERSONAL	*GLOBAL*
Begin to take personal responsibility, develop a plan, and help others do the same.	Every person and nation will be affected.

FACTS AND FIGURES

United States FY 2012
Revenue: $2.45 trillion
Expenses: $3.54 trillion
Deficit: $1.09 trillion
For every $1 received in revenue in FY 2012, the government spent $1.45

U.S. Budget Compared to a Family's Budget
Income: $24,000
Expenses: $35,000
Debt at beginning of year: $148,000
Debt at end of year: $161,000

History of Deficits
Deficits in 36 of last 40 years

National Debt
January 20, 2009: $10.6 trillion
September 30, 2013: $16.7 trillion
Projected for 2017: $20 trillion+
The national debt has not decreased in 56 years

National Debt Milestones

Years to reach milestone of $10 trillion in debt: 233 (1776–2009)

Years to add another $10 trillion to the debt: 8 years or less (2009–2017)

Historical Average Debt Growth Rate

30-year average (1983–2014): 8.68 percent

To whom do we owe the debt?

China: $1.277 trillion (July 2013)

Japan: $1.135 trillion (July 2013)

The U.S. Federal Reserve is purchasing 60 percent to 80 percent of our debt

Interest Paid on the National Debt

FY 2013: $416 billion

Average interest rate on the national debt (September 2013): 2.43 percent

Thirty-year average interest rate (1983–2013): 6.32 percent

Average interest rate on the national debt (October 31, 1981): 11.54 percent

U.S. Monetary Base (money supply)

September 10, 2008: $875 billion

September 18, 2013: $3.546 trillion

2003–2008 Increase: 16.19 percent

2009–2013 Increase: 305 percent

Social Security Trust Fund

There is no money in the Social Security Trust Fund. All cash revenues have been spent and replaced with $2.6 trillion in IOUs.

TALKING POINTS

- America is on an unsustainable fiscal course.

- We are approaching the point of no return when it will become mathematically impossible for our nation to correct the problem.

- Our economic problems are symptoms of our spiritual problems as a nation.

- Both political parties share responsibility for our problem.

- God has not promised perpetual prosperity to any person or nation. Contrary to what some believe, this includes the United States of America.

- Just because a short-term fiscal problem has been solved (debt ceiling raised, unemployment down, housing recovery, or campaign promises to cut the deficit) doesn't mean the real problem has been solved. All of these are just temporary seasons of good economic press releases.

- Long-term deficit spending bankrupts nations. Need two reference points? Ancient Rome and modern-day Greece.

- What caused the Roman demise? Three things: (1) poor fiscal policy; (2) pride; (3) moral decay. In other words, they self-destructed.

- America appears to be using Rome's playbook. We are on the same path.

- Your first priority is to prepare *spiritually*.

- Your second priority is to prepare *financially*.

- The best advice the world is offering is to hoard your resources, buy guns and gold. *We can do better.*

- You can make wise or foolish decisions in any economy.

- You need to have a sense of urgency to put your financial house in order.

- View any peaceful economic months or years ahead as a gift of God's mercy in your life—*allowing you more time to prepare*, both spiritually and financially.

- We must live like the sons of Issachar, "men who understood the times, with knowledge of what Israel should do" (1 Chronicles 12:32).

- Understanding biblical truths are how we begin to understand and frame life events such as life and death; prosperity and poverty; economic expansions and recessions, success and failure; *and yes, even nations rising and falling.*

- People suffer for the sins and mistakes of others.

- The issues of our national debt and runaway deficits are no longer just about your kids and grandkids. It's now about you and me, as well. It doesn't matter if you are twenty, forty, sixty, or eighty years old. The timeline has shifted and we all need to take action.

- We are talking about a global economic storm that will potentially affect billions of people, spiritually and financially.

- When the economic storm comes, we will have the greatest opportunity for ministry in the history of our nation. *But will you be ready? Will your church be ready?*

- Some people will actually profit during and after the economic storm.

- Could God be using the coming economic storm to bring about another great spiritual awakening?

- *PREPARE* is more about you than it is about solving all the problems with the federal government, the president, and Congress.

INDEX OF CHARTS, LISTS, DEFINITIONS, CONCEPTS, AND WEBSITES

Charts

Lists

Definitions

Concepts

Helpful Government Websites

www.treasurydirect.gov

www.GAO.gov

www.SSA.gov

www.CBO.gov

QUOTES

This is preeminently the time to speak the truth, the whole truth, frankly and boldly. Nor need we shrink from honestly facing conditions in our country today.

President Franklin D. Roosevelt, first inaugural address, March 4, 1933

We face the most predictable economic crisis in history.

Erskine Bowles, former chief of staff for President Bill Clinton, testifying before the Senate Budget Committee, March 8, 2011

Any government, like any family, can for a year spend a little more than it earns. But you and I know that a continuation of that habit means the poorhouse.

President Franklin D. Roosevelt, radio address on the National Democratic platform, Albany, NY, July 30, 1932

There are two ways to enslave a nation.
One is by the sword. The other is by debt.

President John Adams (1797–1801)

Albert Einstein said the most powerful force in the universe is compound interest, and today the miracle of compounding interest is working against the federal government.

Government Accountability Office, Long-Term Fiscal Outlook, June 17, 2008

*The single biggest threat to national security
is the national debt.*

Navy Admiral Mike Mullen, chairman of the Joint Chiefs of Staff,
August 26, 2012

*We know from centuries of evidence in countless economies,
from ancient Rome to today's Zimbabwe, that running the
printing press to pay off today's bills leads to much worse problems later on. The inflation that results from the flood
of money into the economy turns out to be far worse than the
fiscal pain those countries hoped to avoid. . . . Failing to face
up to our responsibility will produce the mother of all financial
storms. The warning signs have been flashing for years, but we
find it easier to ignore them than to take action.
Will we take the painful fiscal steps necessary to prevent
the storm by reducing and eventually eliminating our
fiscal imbalances? That depends on you.*

Richard W. Fisher, president of the Federal Reserve Bank of Dallas,
remarks before the Commonwealth Club of California,
San Francisco, May 28, 2008

*We've gotta go spend money to keep from going bankrupt? . . .
Yes, that's what I'm telling you.*

Vice President Joe Biden, July 16, 2009

*The federal government faces increasing pressures yet a shrink-
ing window of opportunity for phasing in adjustments.*

Government Accountability Office, Long-Term Fiscal Outlook,
June 17, 2008

*The passage of time has only worsened the situation:
The size of the challenge has grown and the time to address
it has shrunk. The longer we wait, the more painful and
difficult the choices will become, and the greater
the risk of a very serious economic disruption.*

Government Accountability Office, *Long-Term Fiscal Outlook*,
January 29, 2008

These dates call attention to the narrowing window. . . . Absent action, debt held by the public will grow to unsustainable levels.
Government Accountability Office, Long-Term Fiscal Outlook,
June 17, 2008

The longer action to deal with the nation's long-term fiscal outlook is delayed, the larger the changes will need to be, increasing the likelihood that they will be disruptive and destabilizing.
Government Accountability Office, Long-Term Fiscal Outlook:
Fall 2009 Update

With the passage of time the window to address the long-term challenge narrows and the magnitude of the required changes grows.
Government Accountability Office, Long-Term Fiscal Outlook:
Fall 2010 Update

I place economy among the first and most important virtues, and public debt as the greatest of dangers to be feared. . . . To preserve our independence, we must not let our rulers load us with perpetual debt . . . We must make our choice between economy and liberty or profusion and servitude.
President Thomas Jefferson (1801–1809)

This debt and these deficits that we are incurring on an annual basis are like a like a cancer. And they are truly going to destroy the country from within.
Erskine Bowles, testimony before the Senate Budget Committee,
March 8, 2011

If we do nothing, by the year 2020, we'll be spending over a trillion dollars a year on interest cost alone.
Erskine Bowles, interview with Maria Bartiromo,
November 15, 2012

SCRIPTURES TO STUDY AND MEMORIZE

The wise see danger ahead and prepare;
a fool ignores the facts and suffers the consequences.

Proverbs 27:12

The earth is the Lord's, and all it contains,
The world, and those who dwell in it.

Psalm 24:1

How blessed is the man who does not walk in the
*   counsel of the wicked,*
Nor stand in the path of sinners,
Nor sit in the seat of scoffers!
But his delight is in the law of the Lord,
And in His law he meditates day and night.
He will be like a tree firmly planted by streams of water,
Which yields its fruit in its season
And its leaf does not wither;
And in whatever he does, he prospers.

Psalm 1:1-3

"Therefore everyone who hears these words of Mine and acts on
them, may be compared to a wise man who built his house on
the rock. And the rain fell, and the floods came, and the winds

blew and slammed against that house; and yet it did not fall, for it had been founded on the rock. Everyone who hears these words of Mine and does not act on them, will be like a foolish man who built his house on the sand. The rain fell, and the floods came, and the winds blew and slammed against that house; and it fell—and great was its fall."

Matthew 7:24-27

[We must be like] the sons of Issachar, men who understood the times, with knowledge of what Israel should do.

1 Chronicles 12:32

Iron sharpens iron, so one man sharpens another.

Proverbs 27:17

No one can serve two masters; for either he will hate the one and love the other, or he will be devoted to one and despise the other. You cannot serve God and wealth.

Matthew 6:24

Yet you do not know what your life will be like tomorrow. You are just a vapor that appears for a little while and then vanishes away.

James 4:14

Set your mind on the things above, not on the things that are on earth.

Colossians 3:2

Do not store up for yourselves treasures on earth, where moth and rust destroy, and where thieves break in and steal. But store up for yourselves treasures in heaven, where neither moth nor rust destroys, and where thieves do not break in or steal.

Matthew 6:19-20

Do not be conformed to this world, but be transformed by the renewing of your mind, so that you may prove what the will of God is, that which is good and acceptable and perfect.

Romans 12:2

See to it that no one takes you captive through philosophy and empty deception, according to the tradition of men, according to the elementary principles of the world, rather than according to Christ.

Colossians 2:8

Instruct those who are rich in this present world not to be conceited or to fix their hope on the uncertainty of riches, but on God, who richly supplies us with all things to enjoy.

1 Timothy 6:17

What will it profit a man if he gains the whole world and forfeits his soul? Or what will a man give in exchange for his soul?

Matthew 16:26

Not that I speak from want, for I have learned to be content in whatever circumstances I am. I know how to get along with humble means, and I also know how to live in prosperity; in any and every circumstance I have learned the secret of being filled and going hungry, both of having abundance and suffering need. I can do all things through Him who strengthens me.

Philippians 4:11-13

He who loves money will not be satisfied with money, nor he who loves abundance with its income.

Ecclesiastes 5:10

Consider it all joy, my brethren, when you encounter various trials, knowing that the testing of your faith produces endurance. And let endurance have its perfect result, so that you may be perfect and complete, lacking in nothing.

James 1:2-4

For a righteous man falls seven times, and rises again.

Proverbs 24:16

Better is the poor who walks in his integrity than he who is crooked though he be rich.

Proverbs 28:6

"Beware, and be on your guard against every form of greed; for not even when one has an abundance does his life consist of his possessions." And He told them a parable, saying, "The land of a rich man was very productive. And he began reasoning to himself, saying, 'What shall I do, since I have no place to store my crops?' Then he said, 'This is what I will do: I will tear down my barns and build larger ones, and there I will store all my grain and my goods. And I will say to my soul, "Soul, you have many goods laid up for many years to come; take your ease, eat, drink and be merry."' But God said to him, 'You fool! This very night your soul is required of you; and now who will own what you have prepared?' So is the man who stores up treasure for himself, and is not rich toward God."

Luke 12:15-21

For the love of money is a root of all sorts of evil, and some by longing for it have wandered away from the faith and pierced themselves with many griefs.

1 Timothy 6:10

Be anxious for nothing, but in everything by prayer and supplication with thanksgiving let your requests be made known to God. And the peace of God, which surpasses all comprehension, will guard your hearts and your minds in Christ Jesus.

Philippians 4:6-7

Though the fig tree should not blossom
And there be no fruit on the vines,
Though the yield of the olive should fail
And the fields produce no food,
Though the flock should be cut off from the fold
And there be no cattle in the stalls,
Yet I will exult in the LORD,
I will rejoice in the God of my salvation.
The Lord GOD *is my strength,*
And He has made my feet like hinds' feet,
And makes me walk on my high places.

Habakkuk 3:17-19

*He who is faithful in a very little thing is faithful also in much;
and he who is unrighteous in a very little thing is unrighteous
also in much. Therefore if you have not been faithful in the use of
unrighteous wealth, who will entrust the true riches to you? And
if you have not been faithful in the use of that which is another's,
who will give you that which is your own? No servant can serve
two masters; for either he will hate the one and love the other, or
else he will be devoted to one and despise the other. You cannot
serve God and wealth.*

Luke 16:10-13

Now therefore, thus says the LORD *of hosts, "Consider your ways!
You have sown much, but harvest little; you eat, but there is
not enough to be satisfied; you drink, but there is not enough to
become drunk; you put on clothing, but no one is warm enough;
and he who earns, earns wages to put into a purse with holes."
Thus says the* LORD *of hosts, "Consider your ways!"*

Haggai 1:5-7

*For we have brought nothing into the world, so we cannot take
anything out of it either.*

1 Timothy 6:7

*"Naked I came from my mother's womb,
And naked I shall return there.
The* LORD *gave and the* LORD *has taken away.
Blessed be the name of the* LORD*."*

Through all this Job did not sin nor did he blame God.

Job 1:21-22

Honor the LORD *from your wealth,
And from the first of all your produce.*

Proverbs 3:9

*There is one who scatters, and yet increases all the more,
And there is one who withholds what is justly due,
and yet it results only in want.*

The generous man will be prosperous,
And he who waters will himself be watered.

Proverbs 11:24-25

Give, and it will be given to you. They will pour into your lap
a good measure—pressed down, shaken together, and running
over. For by your standard of measure it will be measured to you
in return.

Luke 6:38

Now this I say, he who sows sparingly will also reap sparingly,
and he who sows bountifully will also reap bountifully. Each one
must do just as he has purposed in his heart, not grudgingly or
under compulsion, for God loves a cheerful giver.

2 Corinthians 9:6-7

And let us not lose heart in doing good, for in due time we shall
reap if we do not grow weary. So then, while we have opportu-
nity, let us do good to all men, and especially to those who are of
the household of faith.

Galatians 6:9-10

Conduct yourselves with wisdom toward outsiders, making the
most of the opportunity.

Colossians 4:5

The rich rules over the poor,
And the borrower becomes the lender's slave.

Proverbs 22:7

He who tills his land will have plenty of food,
But he who follows empty pursuits will have poverty in plenty.

Proverbs 28:19

He has told you, O man, what is good; And what does the Lord
require of you, But to do justice, to love kindness, And to walk
humbly with your God?

Micah 6:8

No soldier in active service entangles himself in the affairs of everyday life, so that he may please the one who enlisted him as a soldier.

2 Timothy 2:4

Steady plodding brings prosperity;
hasty speculation brings poverty.

Proverbs 21:5, TLB

He who loves pleasure will become a poor man;
He who loves wine and oil will not become rich.

Proverbs 21:17

The wise man saves for the future, but the foolish man spends whatever he gets.

Proverbs 21:20, TLB

Divide your portion to seven, or even to eight, for you do not know what misfortune may occur on the earth.

Ecclesiastes 11:2

For we must all appear before the judgment seat of Christ, so that each one may be recompensed for his deeds in the body, according to what he has done, whether good or bad.

2 Corinthians 5:10

Each one of us will give an account of himself to God.

Romans 14:12

Your riches won't help you on Judgment Day; only righteousness counts then.

Proverbs 11:4, TLB

For our citizenship is in heaven.

Philippians 3:20

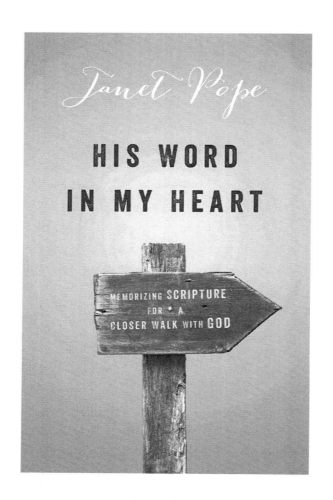

HIS WORD
IN MY HEART

MEMORIZING SCRIPTURE
FOR A
CLOSER WALK WITH GOD

www.JanetPope.org

ACKNOWLEDGMENTS

E very book is a team effort. This book would not be what it is without the help and encouragement I received from a select group of people.

Initial Manuscript Readers

I would like to express my deep appreciation to the following people for giving of their valuable time and spending hours reading the manuscript.

Adam Tarnow
Ed Langton
Janet Pope
Natalie Orr
Paul Allen
Richie Malone
Ron Scarbrough

You read, you prayed, you wrote numerous notes to me in the margins, you asked profound questions, you challenged my thinking, you helped to soften my tone when necessary, you made sure I remained nonpartisan, you kept me focused, you helped me fill in the missing gaps, you helped me delete unnecessary data, you helped me organize, you motivated me, and you helped to make this book the best it could be. You blessed my life and (I hope) the lives of everyone who reads this book. And a big thank you to Cliff Brown and Robert Cornett for giving valuable input.

Publishing Team

Two thumbs up to my publishing team. The quality of this book is a direct reflection of your hard work, creativity, and professionalism. You are the best.

Editor:	Dave Lindstedt
Editorial Consultant:	Natalie Orr
Proofreaders:	Austin Pope
	Paul Allen
	Texas Tucker
Interior Design:	Katherine Lloyd
Cover Design:	Kirk DouPonce

A special thank you to my sister, Martha Ann Simms. Four years ago when *America's Financial Demise* was released, you purchased a case of ninety-six books and passed them out to many of your friends. I still have all the encouraging thank you notes you received and forwarded to me. Thank you for your love, kindness, encouragement and generosity over the years.

My greatest appreciation goes to my wife, Janet.

You are my best friend and most trusted advisor. Thank you for encouraging me to persevere through the thousands of pages of research and numerous manuscripts. *We did it.*

ABOUT THE AUTHOR

Ethan Pope is an author, speaker, and has been a guest on over 700 radio programs. He is a graduate of Dallas Theological Seminary, has taught personal finance classes on the university level, and has spoken at financial seminars across the nation. In 1991 he became a CERTIFIED FINANCIAL PLANNER ™ strictly for educational purposes. Ethan and his wife Janet live in Dallas, Texas, and have two adult children, one son-in-law, and three grandchildren.

Ethan is the author of nine financial books:

How to Be a Smart Money Manager . . . Without Being a Wall Street Wizard (Thomas Nelson Publishers)

The Personal Finance Course: A 12-Week Discipleship Study (Foundations for Living Publications)

There's No Place Like Home: Steps to Becoming a Stay-at-Home Mom by Mary Larmoyeux and Ethan Pope (Broadman & Holman)

Creating Your Personal Money MAP (Tyndale House Publishers)

Cashing It In: Getting Ready for a World Without Money (Moody Publishers)

Social Security? What's In It for You (Moody Publishers)

Identity Theft: Protecting Yourself from an Unprotected World (Moody Publishers)

America's Financial Demise: Approaching the Point of No Return (Intersect Press)

PREPARE: Spiritual and Financial Readiness for the Coming Economic Storm (Intersect Press)

NOTES

1 *Britannica Concise Encyclopedia*; www.merriam-webster.com/dictionary /cognitive%20dissonance.

2 Government Accountability Office, Long-Term Fiscal Outlook, June 17, 2008, GAO-08-912T, 2. Italics added.

3 U.S. Department of Treasury, *Final Monthly Treasury Statement; Fiscal Year 2012*, 2; www.fms.treas.gov/mts/mts0912.pdf.

4 U.S. Department of Treasury, *Final Monthly Treasury Statement; Fiscal Year 2013*, 2; www.fms.treas.gov/mts/mts0913.pdf.

5 See www.cbo.gov budget projection reports for 2013-2023.

6 Franklin D. Roosevelt, radio address on the National Democratic platform, Albany, NY, July 30, 1932; www.presidency.ucsb.edu/ws/?pid=88406.

7 See "A History of Surpluses and Deficits in the United States"; www.davemanuel .com/history-of-deficits-and-surpluses-in-the-united-states.php.

8 www.john-adams-heritage.com/quotes.

9 www.treasurydirect.gov/NP/debt/current.

10 www.treasurydirect.gov/govt/reports/pd/histdebt/histdebt.htm.

11 Government Accountability Office, *The Nation's Long-Term Fiscal Outlook: March 2009 Update* (GAO-09-405SP), 1. Italics added.

12 Ibid. Italics added.

13 Government Accountability Office, *Long-Term Fiscal Outlook* (June 17, 2008, GAO-08-912T), 14.

14 www.treasurydirect.gov/govt/rates/pd/avg/2013/2013_09.htm; www .treasurydirect/gov/govt/reports/ir/ir_expense.htm.

15 www.treasurydirect.gov/govt/reports/pd/mspd/mspd.htm.

16 www.treasurydirect.gov/govt/reports/pd/mspd/mspd.htm. Click on 1981 link, then click on October.

17 Search the Internet for "Federal Reserve purchasing debt" and read the numerous articles available online.

18 Joint Chiefs of Staff, Navy Admiral Mike Mullen, speaking to members of Detroit Economic Club on August 26, 2012 [www.jcs.mil/newsarticle.aspx?ID=360]

19 http://research.stlouisfed.org/publications/mt/notes.pdf

20 Search online for articles about the nation of Zimbabwe.

21 www.research.stlouisfed.org/fred2/series/BASE.txt

22 www.research.stlouisfed.org/fred2/series/BASE.txt

23 www.bea.gov/national/xls/gdplev.xls

24 Richard W. Fisher, "Storms on the Horizon," remarks before the Commonwealth Club of California, San Francisco (May 28, 2008); www.dallasfed.org/news /speeches/fisher/2008/fs080528.cfm.

25 For many years it was a bimetallic (gold and silver) system.

26 The Gold Standard Act of March 14, 1900, officially placed the U.S. on the gold standard: www.treasury.gov/about/history/Pages/1900-present.aspx.

27 The U.S. Treasury Web site lists June 5, 1933, as the official day the U.S. abandoned the gold standard: www.treasury.gov/about/history/Pages/1900-present.aspx.

28 I have included this quote not to be disrespectful to Vice President Biden, but to document that one of our top leaders has acknowledged that our nation is headed toward bankruptcy. Mr. Biden's proposed solution that we spend more money underscores the need for a robust debate about fiscal policy. We must move beyond both political correctness and harsh words and be able to discuss our nation's core values and whether we are headed in the right direction. We should all welcome this debate. (Vice President Biden's remarks were transcribed from www.youtube.com/watch?v=-wPO1xVAO_Y. Italics were added to indicate the inflection of Mr. Biden's spoken remarks.)

29 Government Accountability Office, *Long-Term Fiscal Outlook* (June 17, 2008, GAO-08-912T), 1, emphasis added.

30 According to the GAO's mission statement, they "provide Congress with timely information that is objective, fact-based, nonpartisan, nonideological, fair, and balanced." For more information about the GAO, see www.gao.gov/about /index.html.

31 Government Accountability Office, *Long-Term Fiscal Outlook* (January 29, 2008, GAO-08-411T), 1, emphasis added.

32 Government Accountability Office, *Long-Term Fiscal Outlook* (June 17, 2008, GAO-08-912T), 1, emphasis added.

33 Government Accountability Office, *Long-Term Fiscal Outlook: Fall 2009 Update* (GAO-10-137SP), 1, emphasis added.

34 Government Accountability Office, *Long-Term Fiscal Outlook: Fall 2010 Update* (GAO-11-201SP), 1, emphasis added.

35 http://thoughts.forbes.com/thoughts/economy-thomas-jefferson-i-place-economy

36 Erskine Bowles, testimony before the Senate Budget Committee, March 8, 2011.

37 Erskine Bowles, interview with Maria Bartiromo, "Closing Bell with Maria Bartiromo," CNBC, November 15, 2012; www.cnbc.com/id/49710830.

38 Government Accountability Office, Performance Budgeting: Opportunities and Challenges (September 19, 2002, GAO-02-1106T), 3, emphasis added.

39 Government Accountability Office, The Nation's Long-Term Fiscal Outlook: September 2008 Update (GAO-09-94R), 10, emphasis added.

40 D. L. Moody, *Pleasure & Profit in Bible Study* (Chicago: Fleming H. Revell, 1895), 19-21; http://www.gutenberg.org/files/36655/36655-h/36655-h.htm.

41 Ibid., 140.

42 "Since 1986, the United States has minted one-dollar silver coins called Silver Eagles. Each contains a minimum of one troy ounce of 99.9% pure silver. . . . [Silver Eagles are] legal tender, [and] they're the only silver bullion coins whose weight and purity are guaranteed by the United States Government. They're also the only silver coins allowed in an IRA"; www.usmint.gov/mint_programs /american_eagles/?Action=american_eagle_silver.

43 www.ssa.gov/history/stool.html

44 The Wall Street Journal; 8/3/11; C3, "Central Banks Join Rush to Gold."

45 www.forbes.com/sites/greatspeculations/2013/china-working-quitely-to-buy -up-gold/

46 The Wall Street Journal; 11/4/09; C13, "Gold Hits a Record on India's Big Buy."

47 www.bloomberg.com/news/2013-10-06/gold-befuddles-bernanke-as-central -banks-losses-at-545-billion.html

48 Ibid.

Made in the USA
San Bernardino, CA
25 November 2014